# Fitness
# Evaluation
## *of the* Horse

**Jean-Pierre Hourdebaigt, LMT**

WILEY

Wiley Publishing, Inc.

Howell Book House
Published by Wiley Publishing, Inc., Hoboken, New Jersey

For general information on our other products and services or to obtain technical support please contact our Customer Care Department within the U.S. at (800) 762-2974, outside the U.S. at (317) 572-3993 or fax (317) 572-4002.

Wiley also publishes its books in a variety of electronic formats. Some content that appears in print may not be available in electronic books. For more information about Wiley products, please visit our web site at www.wiley.com.

*Library of Congress Cataloging-in-Publication Data:*
Hourdebaigt, Jean-Pierre.
  Fitness evaluation of the horse / Jean-Pierre Hourdebaigt.
     p. cm.
  Includes index.
  ISBN 978-0-470-19229-0 (alk. paper)
1.  Horsemanship. 2.  Horses—Training. 3.  Physical fitness.  I. Title.
  SF309.H684 2008
  636.1'3—dc22
                                                    2007044695

Printed in China
10  9  8  7  6  5  4  3  2  1

Book design by Erin Zeltner
Cover design by José Almaguer
Book production by Wiley Publishing, Inc. Composition Services

# CONTENTS

## Part III: The Palpation Evaluation Program (PEP)

# LIST OF FIGURES

# FOREWORD

Having known and worked professionally with Jean-Pierre Hourdebaigt for the last several years, I have enjoyed contributing to this project during the last twelve months. Jean-Pierre is a remarkable horseman, possessing a clear understanding of the horse's body, mind, and spirit.

Being an experienced rider and trainer, I feel this book is both educational and inspirational. Jean-Pierre's definitions and explanations of the horse's movements and their relationship to the rider are useful for all levels of riding and have proved to be refreshing new outlook for me. Also, with his great knowledge of the equine anatomy, he has created a simple palpation routine to verify the fitness of our horse's muscular system.

I encourage you to read this book and incorporate it into your daily routine. I am sure you will find it an invaluable tool, which will become a constant reference for you over the years.

Michele M. Grubb
Professional Rider

# ACKNOWLEDGMENTS

My sincere gratitude goes to all the horse people and other professionals who have shared with me their stories, their needs and hopes, and most importantly their knowledge and feedback over the years. This life-sharing experience has been a source of inspiration to me.

For making this publication possible, I specially thank:

Brigitte Hourdebaigt, for making my life a beautiful experience every day.

Michele Grubb, for her valuable professional input and for contributing to the ideas necessary to perfect the REP program in the second part of this book.

Brigitte Hawkins, for her professional talent in taking the photos used in this book.

Jennifer Markee and Emily Marshack, for their equestrian talents and their professional input.

# ANATOMICAL TERMS

To better understand the information and instructions given in this book, here is a list of anatomical terms and their respective definitions.

**Caudal:** in direction of the hinds, the tail; the opposite of cranial.

**Cranial:** in direction of the head; the opposite of caudal.

**Rostral:** equivalent to "cranial" when over the head.

**Distal:** in direction of the extremity of a limb; the opposite of proximal.

**Proximal:** close to the beginning of the limb; the opposite of distal.

**Dorsal:** in direction of the dorso, the upper line of the horse; the opposite of ventral.

**Ventral:** in direction of the abdomen, the lower line; the opposite of dorsal.

**Lateral:** away from the median plane, which divides the body in two parts; the opposite of medial.

**Medial:** close to the median plane, which divides the body in two; the opposite of lateral.

**Palmar:** equivalent to "ventral" when dealing with the foreleg hoof; the opposite of dorsal.

**Plantar:** equivalent to "ventral" when dealing with the hind leg hoof; the opposite of dorsal.

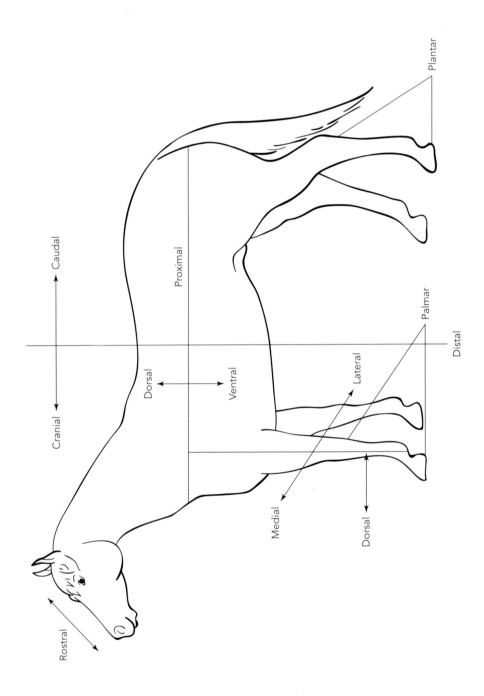

# INTRODUCTION

Horses are a living paradox: they are big and strong, and yet also fragile. Regardless of your professional or amateur status as a horseperson, and which discipline you are involved in, you and your horse will go through a lot of miles together, both in training and in competition. The general objective of this book is to provide you with important knowledge that will help you evaluate your horse's fitness and possibly solve some of the problems he may show. This fitness evaluation program will help you to improve your relationship with your animal in several ways. You will be able to:

❖ Identify the strong and weak areas of your horse.

❖ Better understand your horse's aptitudes.

❖ Select a specific exercise program to balance and strengthen your horse, and progress in your riding performance.

❖ Identify early signs and symptoms of strain in your horse, and therefore prevent complications or injuries.

❖ Better care for your horse.

❖ Save time and money by contacting your veterinarian early in the process.

This fitness evaluation program will also put at your fingertips some simple massage palpation skills to evaluate several key anatomical areas on the horse. Your horse will love you for it. The knowledge gained from this book will allow you to easily and quickly perform your personal evaluation of your horse or any horse, anywhere, and at any time. The expertise gained from this book will save you a lot of time and money as you will be able to evaluate and prevent any problems. This knowledge will be with you for the years to come.

This book has been organized in three parts.

**Part I** gives you important information on how to secure the best conditions to carry out a successful fitness evaluation. You will learn how to develop your hands' palpation skills, how to perform several basic massage movements, and some simple stretching exercises. Valuable information on the horse's musculoskeletal anatomy and on the horse's various stands evaluation is provided to you.

**Part II** offers you a simple Riding Evaluation Program (the REP) to help you evaluate the fitness of the horse at all his normal gaits. This easy step-by-step REP will allow you to identify any abnormalities, if present, in your horse at any gaits. The information contained in this section will help you recognize the stronger and the weaker sides of your horse, and any tight muscle groups or sore joints. As you proceed to work all natural gaits and their variations, you will be able to assess all aspects of his anatomy. As you gain experience with this process, you will make better guesses about what you feel, see, and get from your horse's performance.

**Part III**, the Palpation Evaluation Program (the PEP), will allow you to further your investigation and verify your guesses from the earlier riding evaluation. Down on the ground, this PEP will help you determine what is really showing in your horse's musculoskeletal system. From your riding clues, you will be able to follow up with your fingertips to identify the exact location of any problem. In this section, there is a multi-point diagnostic test for the horse's musculoskeletal system. The valuable information contained here will make you comfortable with carrying out the evaluation of 25 important points on each side of the horse.

The combination of the REP and the PEP will enable you to identify existing musculoskeletal conditions or conformation problems, to evaluate the extent of these conditions or problems, to interpret the results of your examination relevant to the use of the horse, and to identify the potential for future problems. Your personal examination will reveal right away the actual fitness of your horse. In turn, this will allow you to refine your training, or perhaps to seek the help of other professionals.

The knowledge gained from this manual will allow you to carry out your own fitness evaluation on any horse, for years to come. In turn, this will allow you to improve upon your horse's fitness by working in concert with your trainer or your veterinarian.

The valuable educational material contained in this fitness evaluation book will help you discover, or rediscover, all aspects of your horse. In turn it will help you improve his training and performance. In the case of a new horse, it will really help you to choose the right horse for you. The content of this book will help you to think intelligently, save time and money, and improve your horse. I know this book will serve you well.

**Note:** This book is not intended as a substitute for medical advice from a licensed veterinarian. Rather, it is designed to give practical assistance to the horseperson. When in doubt, please contact your veterinarian.

Enjoy your newfound awareness.

Jean-Pierre Hourdebaigt, LMT

# PREPARATION

"Being prepared is half the battle," the old saying goes. The materials presented here prepare you to be ready to ensure the good progression of your horse's fitness evaluation. In order to maximize your work, this part shows you how to develop a good approach and good palpation skills to best evaluate your horse. You will learn some simple massage movements and a short relaxation massage routine, which will be part of the PEP (Palpation Evaluation Program) portion of your horse's fitness evaluation presented in the third part. You will also learn some simple stretching exercises, valuable not only for the evaluation, but also for your horse at all times to keep him flexible and supple. The knowledge gained from this first part will stay with you for the rest of your life.

This section also contains valuable information on your horse's musculoskeletal anatomy and its conformation, as well as on the various stances seen with our equine friends. This will help you develop a sharper eye and better understand a horse's musculoskeletal system.

The knowledge gained from this section prepares you well and builds your confidence to secure the optimal conditions for a successful fitness evaluation of your horse.

# 1

## PALPATION SKILLS

The manner in which you will deal with your horse during your palpation evaluation program is of the utmost importance. You need to secure a good communication with your horse, so use a soft and calming voice to address him and ease him. The quality of your touch is also important. Use a light and soft touch to deliver a comforting feeling as you palpate the various muscle groups and body parts of your horse. Stay relaxed and very attentive to your work. The more relaxed you are, the more relaxed the horse will be and the easier your evaluation will be. This chapter prepares you for this type of work. In order to develop your skills, consider the following points.

## TOUCH

A gentle touch provides comforting feelings to the horse during his evaluation. The caring feeling conveyed to your horse through the soothing contact of your hands will contribute to the relaxation of his nervous system. This smooth approach will positively influence your horse in trusting your work. Therefore, it is very important for you to work on your sense of touch.

First, become aware of the great sensitivity of your hands. The palms of your hands and the pads of your fingertips are equipped with nerve endings that can give you a considerable amount of accurate information about the physiological state of the body part you are working on, helping you considerably in your evaluation of the horse's musculoskeletal structures. Learning to trust your hands is not always an easy process; however, with the right mind-set, you can concentrate and feel all the subtle changes in the various tissues you are working on.

In the early stages of your practice, a very efficient way to develop your perceptions and tactile sensitivity is to spend some time palpating different horses with your eyes closed for short periods of time, and by taking calm, deep breaths. This will help you the most in rapidly developing finger sensitivity. The heightened perception of your fingers is an important key to your palpation skills. The quality of your evaluation work is strongly related to the sensitivity of your hands. For best results in your PEP, develop gentle and skilled hands with sensitive fingertips. The following information on the four T's and on pressure, contact, and rhythm will help you refine your palpation skills.

## THE FOUR T'S

The sensations you perceive through your hands and fingers can be classified into four main categories, referred to as "the four T's": temperature, texture, tension, and tenderness.

### Temperature

The normal body temperature of a horse is 99 to 100.5 degrees Fahrenheit (38 degrees Celsius). Any changes in the temperature of the horse's skin suggest that certain problems may exist. For example, an area that is abnormally cool to the touch compared to the rest of the body is usually indicative of a lack of blood circulation in that area. This may signify problems such as muscle tension, possible presence of scar tissue, soreness, and eventually pain.

An area that is warm to the touch indicates the presence of inflammation, and is a sure sign of an underlying problem, such as a stress point, trigger point, or some form of trauma (bruise, overuse) and an associated level of pain and muscular compensation.

Mild variations in local body temperature may be the warning signs of more serious problems. When in doubt, contact your veterinarian.

### Texture

Texture of the tissues refers to the density and the elasticity of the skin, the fascial tissue, and muscle fibers. During your palpation, be sure you are not palpating directly over a bony area (over the scapular spine of the scapula, for example). Do practice with healthy animals first in order to develop a feel for healthy tissue, so you will know better what is normal and what is abnormal.

On a relaxed horse, the tissue texture should be soft and pliable. It should not be hard, hot, or tender to your horse (see next paragraph). The hardening of a tissue is a sign of an underlying problem. The hardness may feel different under your fingertips depending on its location. It may feel like leather over a large surface, a lump over a smaller area, or like piano wires stretching out to other areas. Hardness is a definite sign that underlying problems such as muscle spasms, stress points, trigger points, or fascial restrictions have developed. Tissues that feel either too soft or puffy indicate the presence of swelling. Edema, another term for swelling, results from the presence of excessive lymphatic fluid and is a sign of congestion and/or of an underlying inflammatory condition. When palpating puffy tissues it is important to understand why they might be puffy. For instance, if you feel puffiness over the withers, it might be indicative of a saddle fitting issue, where some puffiness in the lower leg of an older horse is quiet normal. If you do not have a simple explanation for the presence of that swelling, contact your veterinarian.

## Tenderness

Tenderness of the structures refers to the degree of sensitivity from the horse to your touch. Regardless of the tissue you are working on, whether muscles, tendons, ligaments, or joints, if the horse's sensitivity is high, it is a sure sign of an underlying problem.

Tenderness shows that the nerve endings are irritated or perhaps even damaged. The horse's reaction to your touch is proportional to the degree of severity of that condition and of his stress level. This is why I always recommend you start your palpations with a very light touch. If excessive tenderness is present during your palpation, consult your veterinarian for proper diagnosis.

## Tension

Tension refers to the high tonus of the muscle fibers. Muscle tension is often the result of too much exercise. Sometimes muscle tension can result from trauma and associated scar tissue buildup (posttrauma) and fascial restrictions. Too much tightness means less blood circulation, less nutrients, and less oxygen to the affected area, thus delaying the healing of the tissues. Tension will increase toxin buildup, creating an underlying inflammation. Trigger points (lactic acid buildups, a by-product of energy burning) and stress points (small spasms) may result. It is normal to expect some high muscle tone immediately after exercise. To find tension in the muscle fibers after a good rest is a sure sign of some muscular compensation secondary to another problem. As you palpate the horse musculature, you should feel the same muscle tone continuously, from the neck to the back and over the four limbs. Any area where the muscle fibers feel more contracted is an indication of muscle compensation.

Thus, when you start your palpation evaluation, always use your fingers as sensors to get feedback (the four T's) on the condition of the horse you are working on. Think of your fingers as probes. Let them feel and assess what they touch. You will be amazed to find how fast this heightened perception will develop in you, especially if you keep practicing your smooth breathing and focused attention. Your fingers should become an extension of your brain.

## PRESSURE, CONTACT, AND RHYTHM

Another important key to a successful palpation evaluation is mastering your pressure, your contact, and your rhythm as you assess your horse. The more flowing you are with these three factors, the more enjoyable your work will be to the horse, allowing him to better relax and trust the process.

### Pressure

The pressure used during a palpation evaluation is very gentle. The fluidity of the movements coupled with light pressure allows for better relaxation.

First, familiarize yourself with your strength at home. Use a kitchen or bathroom scale to practice evaluating your force. Practice pushing between 1 and 3 pounds of pressure, then 5 or 10 pounds of pressure, and up to 15 or 20 pounds of pressure. You will be amazed to find how quickly pressure builds up, and realize how little exertion you need in order to reach deep into the muscular structures. Repeat this exercise until you have developed a feel for what it takes for you to reach any desired level of pressure. Practice with different strokes, by using one thumb, two thumbs, the fingers of one hand, the fingers of both hands, the palm of the hand, two palms, simultaneously or alternately, etc. Be creative! You need to be confident in your ability to apply any desired amount of pressure.

During a palpation evaluation, you will mostly use pressure between 0.5 pound and 3 pounds, sometimes 5 depending on the location you are working on. Make sure the horse is fine with it. However, if your horse appears tender over the area you are working on, you need to back down to a lighter pressure ranging from 0.1 to 1 pound of pressure. Remember, a horse can feel a fly landing on his back!

When dealing with scar tissue restrictions over an area, use only a pressure that you feel allows you to reach the firmness of those restrictions. Indeed, the best way to know is to closely observe your horse's feedback signs, especially his eyes. With practice, you will instinctively know the pressure needed without causing discomfort.

**Note:** Always keep in mind that above 25 pounds of pressure there is a risk of bruising the soft tissues (muscles). This won't be noticed since a bruise can't be seen under the horse's coat. Usually the presence of a bruise is indicated by a slight hardening of the tissues, caused by blood and lymph congestion, and the tenderness of these tissues on palpation shortly after your session.

Too much pressure is counterproductive during a palpation evaluation. Excessive pressure will irritate the nerve endings present in the tissue you are working on, sending referred pain throughout the entire area. This will cause your horse to tense up, and not cooperate.

Keep in mind that, as with people, some horses prefer a deeper and heavier approach to touch, and some prefer a lighter and softer touch. You will be able to clue in to your animal's tolerance by starting slowly and gently first to trigger a relaxing sensation. It is always safe to begin with a light pressure and work progressively into the release. Never jab your fingers into the animal's flesh. Start with light contact and build up your pressure slowly as you move over the tissues as explained in chapter 2, the SEW and WES approach. This progressive approach will prevent the horse from tensing up and trying to get away from you. Do not get carried away while working. Constantly assess your horse's eyes and his feedback signs. Tune into the four T's and "listen" to your fingers. Pain and discomfort should always be considered as a warning signal. Be attentive, constantly adjusting the pressure of your technique.

## Contact

To maximize the quality of your touch and hand contact with the horse, keep your hands flexible at all times, molding them to his body parts. Always remember that your hands are your point of contact with your animal. Much information passes through your hands, both to you and to the animal. At the same time, your skilled hands perceive important feedback signs (the four T's) and give your horse a nice sensation of comfort and care. A mindful contact will be strongly perceived by the animal, strengthening his trust in your work. You should feel a lot of warmth and lots of energy flowing through your hands during your contact. This deeper sense of contact will give you much feedback on what is happening with your horse as you are progressing with your palpation evaluation.

As you always begin with light pressure, your molding hands will give your horse a pleasurable sensation of comfort. Then as you gently build your pressure to the point where you meet the desired structures, the comforting touch will relax your horse and help him accept the soreness sometimes associated with this process. Then as you progressively release your pressure, the same comforting touch will give your horse a feeling of continuity, ensuring connection and comfort.

## Rhythm

In this context, rhythm refers to the frequency at which you carry out the different movements involved in your palpation evaluation. Rhythm plays a strong factor in the effectiveness of your session. As a rule, the rhythm of application should be twenty strokes per minute for a slow rhythm, sixty strokes per minute (one per second) for a gentle rhythm, and eighty to ninety strokes per minute for a faster, stimulating rhythm.

Use the gentle rhythm to start your session, to weave your moves into one another, and to finish your work, especially when using effleurage or stroking moves over an area. A faster rhythm often stimulates and irritates a horse and is counterproductive to the good application of your palpation evaluation. (It is only used when you need to stimulate a horse, before exercising, for example).

A soothing rhythm works best in relaxing the horse's nervous system, and assists you in gaining his confidence with your work. Yet this soft approach allows you to apply any technique you need.

## ATTITUDE

Before you proceed with your palpation evaluation, it is important to quiet your mind. Become focused and attentive, constantly assessing the sensations your fingers give you, the four T's, as well as the feedback signs shown by your horse (feedback signs are discussed later in this chapter).

Do not let your mind wander away. We have a tendency to let our left brain dominate our thoughts, leading to rationalization and criticism, and thereby reducing our perceptions. By practicing relaxation through breathing, we allow the right brain to dominate, giving us more nonverbal intuition. Taking gentle and regular deep breaths will bring this harmony and help you stay focused yet relaxed. This calm approach will heighten your perceptions and give you a more refined touch. When you allow both hemispheres of your brain to function in harmony, the balance will enhance your perception and effectiveness. This will contribute to a clearer perception of the tactile feedback received from your fingertips. Repeatedly take gentle long breaths. This sense of calm will allow you to better feel the structures you touch. A calm and focused presence while working around you horse will promote a positive relationship between you and your horse.

## OBSERVATION

Develop a keen sense of observation, a sharp eye you can use to detect any musculoskeletal asymmetries in the horse's posture both at rest and when moving or playing (You will learn more about the musculoskeletal system in chapter 5). You should first look at the horse globally, comparing the various body parts in relation to one another: size, proportion, and alignment. Get a general impression of the horse's state of health and fitness, the quality of his coat and of the muscular structure and tone, section by section. Chapter 6 gives you valuable information on the various horse stances. Also, observe the various gaits: walk, trot, and canter.

Look for any abnormalities, restrictions, or signs of discomfort. This simple observation can reveal a lot to you.

# RECOGNIZING SIGNS OF INFLAMMATION

As you carry out your massage palpation evaluation routine, it is important to be able to recognize the various signs of an inflammation. An inflammation is a natural body process that serves to destroy, dilute, or wall off both the injurious agent and the injured tissues so that repair may be effective. The classical signs of inflammation are:

❖ Pain
❖ Heat
❖ Redness (not often seen under the hair)
❖ Swelling
❖ Loss of function (immobility)

There are three basic phases of inflammation:

**The first phase** is also known as the acute phase. The inflammatory process begins with a short vasoconstriction quickly followed by a vasodilation with an increase in vascular permeability (swelling). Usually the first twenty-four hours following an injury are considered the acute phase. Keep in mind that an old injury can flare up and show symptoms similar to an acute phase.

**The second phase** is also known as the subacute phase. During that phase, the vascular permeability is sustained with phagocytes (cells that ingest and destroy microbes and debris) that migrate to the injury site causing:

• An increase in swelling
• An oxidation of fluid from the vessels
• Clustering of local sites along the vessel wall
• Phagocytosis of microorganisms
• Disposal of the accumulated toxins and debris by macrophage

This phase usually lasts between twenty-four and seventy-two hours.

**The third phase** is also known as the chronic phase. During that phase the repair process begins with:

• Deposition of fibrin in the vessels
• Migration of fibroblast cells to the area
• Development of new, normal tissue cells

Usually past seventy-two hours is considered the chronic phase. Proportional to the severity of the injury, a chronic phase can last weeks, or sometimes months. In some instances, a chronic injury can flare up, displaying signs similar to the ones seen in an acute phase (swelling and tenderness).

The nature and severity of the problem causing the inflammation will strongly influence the span of the different phases of that particular inflammation.

When facing an acute stage of inflammation, contact your veterinarian immediately for proper diagnosis and course of action. Remember, an inflammation is a sign the horse is experiencing some degree of discomfort. When dealing with a chronic inflammation, see chapter 15, page 150, to familiarize yourself with the list of contraindications to massage palpation and make sure that none applies. When in doubt, contact your veterinarian.

## SUMMARY

With proper preparation and practice you will soon develop an inner appreciation of the feedback received from your fingertips and will know exactly how to adjust to the right pressure, right contact, and right rhythm. Developing your four T's awareness will help you pick up signs of inflammation anywhere on the horse. Coupled with your knowledge of the structures you are working on (chapter 5) and the different approach techniques (chapter 2), plus a strong dose of common sense, you will soon master harmoniously the three dimensions of pressure, contact, and rhythm.

Remember, practice makes perfect. As you absorb the material presented in the third part of this book, try to evaluate as many horses as you can to sharpen your skills. Soon it will become second nature.

# 2

## MASSAGE AWARENESS FOR YOUR PALPATION EVALUATION

This chapter introduces some basic massage movements and combinations that you should use for your palpation evaluation. To teach you in-depth knowledge of equine massage movements, techniques, and routines is beyond the scope of this book; however, you are invited to pick up the book *Equine Massage: A Practical Guide*, Second Edition, from the same author and publisher.

## MASSAGE MOVEMENTS

For a smooth development of your palpation evaluation, the following massage movements should be used: stroking, effleurage, kneading, wringing, skin rolling, and frictions.

Each massage movement can be performed in either a soothing or a stimulating manner, as discussed in chapter 1. As a rule, the rhythm of application should be one stroke per second to maintain a gentle rhythm.

Some of the movements appear very similar, but they all offer specifics of which you need to be aware. This knowledge will help you become an expert in choosing the right massage move to suit the necessary approach. With practice this will become second nature to you. Remember that each massage movement helps you "feel" the structures you work on, and therefore gives you tremendous feedback (the four T's, see chapter 1). Due to the sensitivity of your horse, always start with a light touch before increasing pressure or rhythm.

### STROKING

Stroking is used for its soothing, relaxing, and calming effect on the body, directly affecting the central nervous system. It is the main move used in the relaxation massage routine. When the horse is very nervous, stroking

*2.1 Stroking Massage Movement*

his back and legs will soothe and "ground" him. You always start or finish a massage routine or treatment by applying several strokes over the body part that has been worked on. Also use stroking to weave together various massage techniques, or when moving from one area of the body to another.

Stroking movements are performed in a relaxed, superficial manner with the tips of the fingers or the palms of the hands, very lightly. When stroking, use very light pressure, from 0.1- to 0.5-pound pressure. This is a pure nervous reflex move, so there is no need for mechanical pressure. Stroking can be done in any direction, but preferably along the length of the muscles, following the direction in which the hair lies.

## EFFLEURAGE

Effleurage is the move you will use the most. Effleurage is used as every second move (every ten to twenty seconds) during most of the massage work to emphasize proper drainage. After stroking, it is used to start, weave, or terminate any massage work. To assist the natural flow of the venous blood circulation, always perform effleurage toward the heart.

Effleurage is a gliding movement done with the fingers and palms of the whole hand. During an effleurage stroke, the thumb never leads the hand; rather, it follows the fingers. The hand should be well molded and in full contact with the body part being massaged. You can use one or two hands, simultaneously or alternately, in an even gliding movement. The pressure is usually even throughout the entire stroke, except for

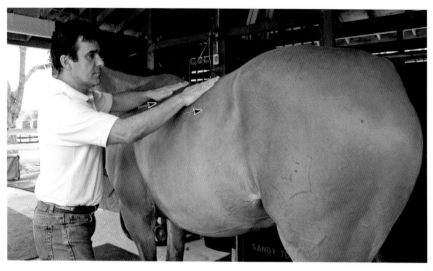

2.2 *Effleurage Massage Movement*

example, when going over bony processes such as the scapular ridge, point of the hip, or point of the elbow or hock.

Effleurage, with its pressure, has a mechanical draining effect on body fluids such as blood and lymph. This draining effect is proportional to the pressure applied and the rhythm of the movement. The best rhythm for effleurages is about twenty strokes per minute on average (one stroke every two or three seconds). A faster rhythm, one or two strokes per second, has a more invigorating effect.

When doing effleurage on a narrow area (for example, the lower legs), use mostly the palmar region of the fingers instead of the whole hand. Adjust the pressure corresponding to the structure being worked on. Work lightly over ligaments and bony structures to avoid triggering soreness, but more heavily over muscle groups to assist the drainage of all the fibers.

Always perform effleurage toward the heart so as to assist the natural flow of the venous blood circulation.

## WRINGING UP

Wringing up is a great move to use on the back, the neck, the shoulders, and the hindquarters. Wringing up efficiently increases the circulation, improves the oxygenation, and removes toxins. It is very useful in reducing inflammation over the muscles of the back and horses love it!

Wringing up is done with the palmar surface of the hand, thumbs abducted at a 90-degree angle. Apply both hands flat on the body part, then start wringing the muscle side to side, almost in the same way you would wring wet linens. The muscle is lightly and gently lifted, then

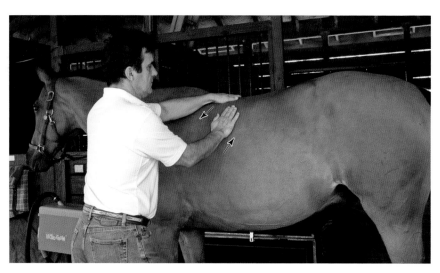

*2.3 **Wringing Up Movement***

wrung side to side. You might think it sounds painful, but on the contrary it feels quiet nice. Try it on your own leg and you will see.

Wringing up is very efficient in stimulating the circulation and warming up muscle groups in a short time. Wringing up can be applied anywhere on the horse's body. Use an average pressure, starting at about 2 pounds and building up to 15 pounds, depending on the muscle mass worked on. Remain light when going over bony areas such as the spine, the scapula, the point of shoulder, or the point of the hip. Your rhythm should be smooth, one stroke per second or less on average. A faster rhythm of two strokes per second will be very stimulating and may be irritating to the horse.

## KNEADING

Kneading is a very effective technique performed with the thumbs or the palmar surface of the three fingertips (index, major, and ring finger). It is done in a rhythmical, circular way (small half circles overlapping one another, pushing outward), the same way you would knead dough. Contact is maintained at all times.

When kneading, the tissues are intermittently compressed against the underlying bone structure. To relax the horse, the rhythm should be one movement per second. Kneading will have a pumping effect, which boosts the circulation, improves the oxygenation, and helps remove toxins from the tissues. It gives in-depth touch to the various bundles of muscle fibers, separating them, draining them, and cleansing them from toxin buildup. Kneading will help you feel scar tissue patches or small spasms (stress points).

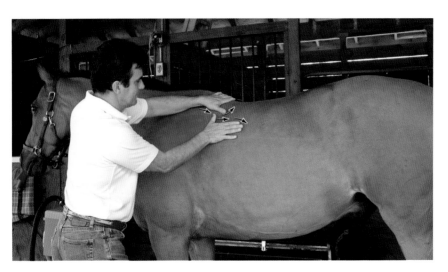

*2.4  Petrissage: Kneading Movement*

Kneading is usually performed with two hands, but it may be performed with one hand when the area being treated is small (the flexor tendon, for example). You can try other combinations using only two fingers or a thumb and fingers. When dealing with large areas (the hind legs, for example), use the full palms of your hands. It is very efficient and it will save wear and tear on your thumbs.

When kneading, gauge your pressure. Start at 2 or 3 pounds. Increase to between 5 and 12 pounds when working the big bulky muscle groups. Intersperse your kneading with a good deal of effleurages every ten to twenty seconds.

## SKIN ROLLING

Skin rolling is a very soothing manipulation, which is used mostly to keep the dermal (skin) layer rich in blood. Skin rolling is used mostly to maintain a healthy and shiny coat, break down little fatty deposits, prevent the formation of excess adhesions, and maintain good elasticity of the skin. Used during your palpation evaluation, it will help you find areas of adhesions.

With thumbs on one side and fingers on the other, grasp and lift the tissues. Using one or both hands (preferably both), push the thumbs forward, rolling the skin toward the fingers. The fingers draw the skin toward the thumbs, lifting, stretching, and squeezing the tissues.

Skin rolling is a gliding motion of the superficial tissues (skin and fat). It should be performed in a slow, soothing manner to avoid irritating the skin nerve endings, especially over areas where the tissues lie tightly on the underlying structures. The angle of direction may be varied and

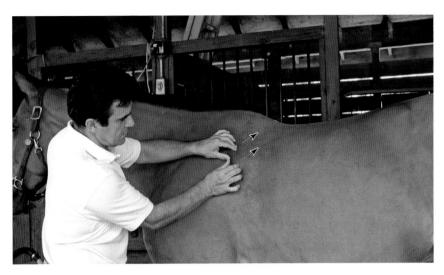

*2.5  Skin Rolling Movement*

repeated to ensure maximum effect to the tissues. This is a great technique to enhance nerve and blood circulation. Use only 2 or 3 pounds pressure maximum.

## FRICTION

Friction can be performed in several ways: with the thumb, the fingers, or the whole hand. This very specific movement is mostly used in sports therapy to break down adhesions developing over muscular fibers, tendons, ligaments, fascia, joint capsules, and bones. However, for your palpation evaluation, friction, especially the double-hand friction movement, will help you quickly assess the tone of the muscle groups.

Always warm up the area thoroughly with the SEW approach (Stroking, Effleurages, and Wringing; see page 17), before proceeding to frictions.

Frictions consist of small, deeper movements applied across the length of the muscle fiber bundle. Use the tip of your thumb, as shown in figure 2.6, or the first three fingers of your hand to friction small, local areas, as shown in figure 2.7.

Use both hands to friction large areas. The double-hand friction movement is performed with both hands side by side, applying a downward pressure with the fingertips right into the muscle, as shown in figure 2.8.

Then, moving slowly and in a motion perpendicular to the muscle fibers, apply friction movements with your fingertips to the entire length of the muscle. With any of these friction movements, expect to see a lot of loose hair being removed.

*2.6 **Thumb Friction Movement***

Position yourself properly, with your shoulders relaxed, elbows slightly flexed, with your wrists positioned in the continuity of the forearms. Your fingers should be at a 90-degree angle to your hands. It is the extension-flexion movement of the fingers that produces the strumming motion.

Now, depending on the amount of tension and, possibly, the level of inflammation within the muscle fibers, your horse might not be comfortable with this technique. When you start the double-hand friction technique using a light pressure, there is an associated sensation of

*2.7 **Hand Friction Movement***

*2.8 **Double-Hand Friction Movement***

"well-being," but as you progress deeper, the sensation might change and become more acute. Stay aware, stay gentle, and proceed cautiously. Monitor your horse's feedback signs, especially his eyes, throughout the entire process. Always position yourself properly so you can see your horse's head ands his eyes. Constantly reassure the horse with your caring voice. Proceed gently, starting with a light 2-pound pressure and progressively increase the pressure to 5 pounds. You can increase up to 10 pounds of pressure when working on large muscle groups such as the extensor and flexor muscle of the neck, the back muscles, and the gluteals or hamstrings of the hinds.

## THE SEW/WES APPROACH

This technique is very important in massage work, because it gives the proper approach for warming up and for draining any area you wish to work on. The title of this technique is made up of two acronyms. SEW stands for Stroking, Effleurage, and Wringing, while WES stands for Wringing, Effleurage, and Stroking.

The SEW approach is used to start and progressively warm up any area you are to massage. Always start with very light and gentle stroking over the area you will be massaging. Then follow with two to three effleurage passes to thoroughly cover the entire area, all along draining toward the heart. Now apply gentle wringing (two passes back and forth) over the whole area. Follow with a set of effleurages and continue with either kneading and/or gentle friction, depending on the nature of your goals. Remember to intersperse with effleurages every twenty seconds.

The WES approach is used when you are finished working an area. This approach will allow you to properly and progressively move out of the area you worked on, ensuring proper drainage. After the last set of effleurages, apply a gentle set of wringing over the entire area worked on (two passes back and forth). Follow with extra effleurages (twice as many as usual, four to six passes) to thoroughly drain the tissues you have massaged. With each effleurage pass you should release your pressure a little, starting around 5 pounds and ending with 2 pounds. Then finish with a light stroking, covering the entire area.

The last bit of stroking in the WES approach can become the opening stroke of the SEW approach to the area you will massage next.

## SUMMARY

A good understanding of the various basic massage movements and their proper applications will contribute greatly to the smoothness of your palpation evaluation program application. Practice makes perfect. It is highly recommended to massage many horses in the manner described here to develop and master your massage skills. Within a few weeks you will feel very proficient at this.

With the knowledge of the equine structures gained from chapter 5, these massage skills will allow you to flow from one body part to another in a harmonious way. When you learn the material presented in part III of this book, you will be more relaxed and confident in the application of the PEP.

# 3

## THE RELAXATION
## MASSAGE ROUTINE

The purpose of the relaxation routine is to relax the animal in a gentle and yet efficient way. There is a great advantage to using the relaxation massage routine prior to your palpation evaluation program, as it will make the horse more compliant with your work.

The relaxation massage routine concentrates on the nervous system only, using mostly pure nervous reflex massage moves over key areas of the spinal column—the poll of the neck, the back, the sacrum, and the tail—to elicit a parasympathetic nervous response in the autonomic nervous system of the animal. The autonomic nervous system ensures the functioning of the horse's nervous system, governing the vital organs and their complex functions. The autonomic nervous system has two major divisions: the sympathetic division and the parasympathetic division. Both originate in the brain. The sympathetic division causes the body to respond to danger, adversity, stress, anger, and pleasure by increasing the heart rate, blood pressure, and blood flow for better oxygen exchange in the muscles. The sympathetic division is responsible for the horse's "fight or flight" reaction. The parasympathetic division monitors body functions during time of rest, sleep, digestion, and elimination, when the body is not ready to go into action. General stimulation of the parasympathetic division promotes relaxation and unconscious functions of the body—breathing, digestion, circulation, immune response, and reproduction.

This relaxation massage routine is specifically designed to stimulate the parasympathetic response.

The routine requires very little pressure, a maximum of 1 or 2 pounds of pressure and a smooth slow rhythm of one move per second. This routine will achieve positive results from the first application.

This relaxation massage routine can be applied at any time: before and after traveling; before, during, and after competition; in the event of a scare; or even when the animal has become restless from boredom. It is recommended before any type of massage work. It will give a complete feeling of relaxation to the horse.

Before beginning this routine, it is important to stand beside the horse for a few minutes to connect with him. Spend a few moments gently stroking the horse's lower neck, progressively stroking upward toward the upper neck and the base of the ears.

***Important note:*** Unfortunately, some horses have a natural aversion to being touched over their poll and ears. A horse afflicted with equine temporomandibular joint dysfunction syndrome (ETDS) will be very protective of his upper neck, especially by the poll area, the ears, and the temporomandibular joints. He might not want your hands over these areas right away. In that case, start right away with some light stroking movements along the back of the horse. Over a period of time, as the horse gets used to your work and builds his trust in you, you will be able to progressively approach his upper neck area. Patience, love, and kindness do wonders for a horse in this situation.

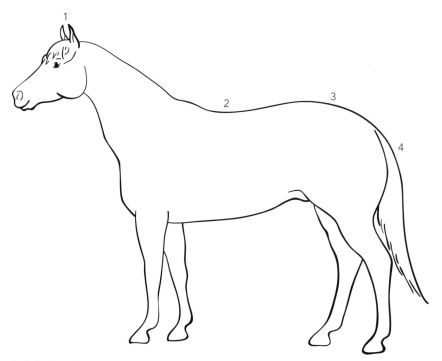

*3.1 **Relaxation Massage Routine Outline, Short Version: (1) Poll Work, (2) Back Work, (3) Sacrum Work, (4) Tail Work***

# RELAXATION MASSAGE ROUTINE

## POLL WORK

After spending a few moments connecting with the horse, offer your left hand opened so the horse lowers his head while you gently bring your right hand to the base of its neck. Then, using stroking or light effleurage movements, bring your right hand to the poll. Using a very light touch, 1 pound of pressure, start applying three clockwise, then twelve counterclockwise gentle small circular movements with the fingertips or the palm of your hand, just behind the ears, as shown in figure 3.2, to trigger the parasympathetic nervous response that allows relaxation.

To reinforce the "let go" atmosphere, talk to your horse quietly. The horse will probably lower his head as a response to your work.

## BACK WORK

Next, follow with two or three light long strokes over the entire back, from withers to the back, as shown in figure 3.3. Use a very light pressure of about 1 or 2 pounds maximum. Your rhythm should be very smooth.

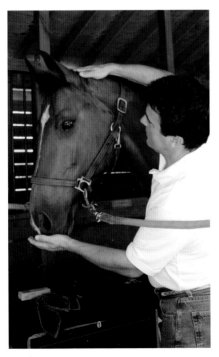

3.2 *Poll Work*

3.3 *Back Work*

## Sacrum Work

As you finish your back work, place your right hand over the sacrum bone. Hold it there with a light vibration for ten to twenty seconds. Then, slowly make three clockwise circular motions, reversing to counterclockwise motions for fifteen to twenty circles, as shown in figure 3.4.

Do not pick up speed as you apply those circles. Keep your rhythm smooth to give a continuous feeling of relaxation. This particular approach will strongly stimulate the parasympathetic nervous response of healing and repair.

## Tail Work

When done with the sacrum work, replace your right hand with your left hand on top of the sacrum to maintain that warm contact with the horse. Then with your right hand, gently pick up the tail by grabbing it a few inches from its base, and bringing it upward, as shown in figure 3.5.

Next, bring the tail into a question mark position, as shown in figure 3.6. Use your left hand to help stretch the tail into a question mark. Hold it in that stretch for five seconds and release.

Next, gently move the tail in a circle, three times clockwise and three times counterclockwise, as shown in figure 3.7. Take note of any movement restriction on either side of the tail; this is a sign of muscle tension in the tail muscles and the hindquarters.

*3.4  Sacrum Work*

*3.5  Raising the Tail Movement*        *3.6  Question Mark Movement*

*3.7  Turning Tail Movement*

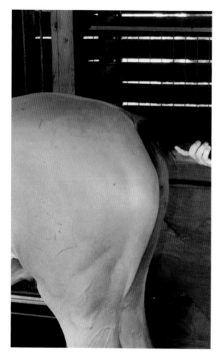

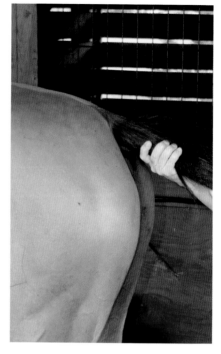

*3.8  Stretching the Tail Out*          *3.9  Squeezing Each Tail Vertebra*

At this point, move yourself to the rear of the horse and pull on his tail very gently, as shown in figure 3.8.

Hold this stretch for approximately thirty seconds to a minute, unless the horse shows signs of discomfort. Usually the horse responds positively by pulling against your traction. Stretching the tail will tremendously contribute to increasing the horse's relaxation.

While stretching the tail with one hand, use the other hand's thumb and fingers to very gently work each vertebra from the base of the tail downward with a few gentle muscle squeezings, as shown in figure 3.9. Reverse the hands if you prefer.

Take note of the tail's flexibility, any tender spots or points of possible inflammation. Release the tail stretch progressively and then stroke the hindquarters and sacrum area for a few seconds.

## SUMMARY

The short version of the relaxation massage routine is a great tool to relax your horse in a very gentle, quick, and efficient way. Learn it and you can apply it at any time, either prior to your palpation evaluation program or before transport, or when at a show. It will relax the horse and make him more compliant with your work.

# 4

Stretching your horse during your palpation evaluation program is very advantageous. The many benefits of stretching range from improving the horse's flexibility and coordination, to preventing muscle problems and providing relaxation.

Stretching will also give you feedback on the horse's physical condition, flexibility, or lack thereof. During these stretches, observe the quality of the motion as well as the horse's reaction to your work. Pay attention to all details. With practice you will quickly see that a stretch reveals a lot of hidden information, not only about the muscles, tendons, or ligaments, but also about the joints and the horse's ability to coordinate himself or not.

Do both forelegs and hind legs stretch similarly? Is one particular stretch causing a reaction? Are the ranges of motion even? Is the horse comfortable overall or not? Is the neck bending on both sides evenly? Is the back supple? Is the tail loose or contracted? All information gathered during your stretching session is an important revelation on how the horse really is at that moment!

*Important note:* Make allowances for a horse that has never been stretched before. He might resist you some during the development part of the stretches, wondering what you are doing to him. Also, young horses might be worried because of their lack of sturdy balance. Proceed gently and comfort the horse by talking to him as you perform the stretches. Usually after two or three tries the horse complies nicely. If he does not, it is probably due to some discomfort elicited by the stretch, thus indicating you some potential problem area.

## HOW TO STRETCH

To attain best results, you need to respect the structures you are working on. To stretch correctly, it is important to be concerned with the animal's natural body alignment. Always move and stretch the horse's limb in their natural range of motion. Do not exert torque or abnormal twist.

Stretching is not a contest to see how far you can stretch. Let the horse show you how loose or how tight he is with each of his body parts.

Stretching should always be done in a relaxed and steady manner. The first time you stretch the horse, do it slowly and gently. The quality of the stretch reveals how the horse feels about the part being stretched. Give the horse time to adjust his body and mind to the physical and the nervous stress release that the stretch initiates.

Note that many horses show varying degrees of sensitivity to handling. Be gentle from the beginning. Make a distinction between a reaction to pain and an objection to handling.

## THE EASY STRETCH

Always start with the easy stretch. The easy stretch means stretching only 75 to 80 percent of the total stretching capability of that particular body part and holding it only for ten seconds. Your horse will enjoy this gentle approach. Be steady in the development of your work. Never work hastily or with jerky movements.

## THE DEEPER STRETCH

Once the horse relaxes into an easy stretch, you can work into the deeper stretch. Past the initial ten seconds and as the muscle tightness decreases, adjust your traction until you again feel a mild tension. Hold for another five seconds.

## THE SPONTANEOUS STRETCH

Often during the deeper stretch and sometimes right away during the easy stretch, the horse will spontaneously stretch himself fully for a few seconds (three to five seconds). This is a definite sign that the animal is enjoying the stretch and needs it very much. As you hold the limb during such spontaneous release, you can feel all the deep tension coming out as a vibration; it is quite an experience. After such a release, there is no need to hold the stretch any longer.

## THE FORELEG STRETCHES

There are three foreleg stretches: the forward stretch, the backward stretch, and the shoulder rotation. Pay attention and make mental notes for each stretch, so that when you stretch the opposite foreleg you can compare and appreciate whether both are even. In case they are not even, you will know which one of the two legs is more restricted and in which way.

### The Forward Stretch

This protraction movement will stretch the muscle involved in the retraction of the foreleg. Pick up the leg above the fetlock with one hand, and place the other behind the elbow. Gently bring the leg forward and upward, as shown in figure 4.1. This stretch will affect the muscles of the shoulder, the trapezius, the rhomboideus, the latissimus dorsi, the serratus cervicis, the deltoideus, and the triceps.

Once the horse is well into the stretch, maintain the tension with one hand behind and above the fetlock, and with your other hand extend the hoof, as shown in figure 4.2. This action will deepen the stretch of the flexor tendons. Be gentle and cautious.

### The Backward Stretch

The retraction movement will stretch the muscles involved in the protraction of the foreleg. With one hand, pick up the leg above the hoof. Place the other hand in front of the canon bone. Gently bring the leg backward until the radius bone is slightly past the 90-degree angle with the ground, as shown in figure 4.3. This is a good stretch for the muscle of the chest and the upper leg, specifically the pectorals, the brachiocephalicus, the biceps, and the extensors.

Once the horse is well into the stretch, maintain the tension with one hand in front and above the fetlock, and with your other hand flex the hoof, as shown in figure 4.4. This action will deepen the stretch of the extensor tendons. Be gentle and cautious.

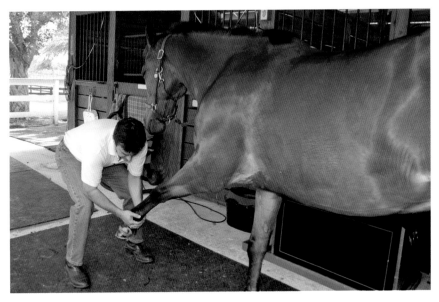

*4.1 Foreleg Forward Easy Stretch*

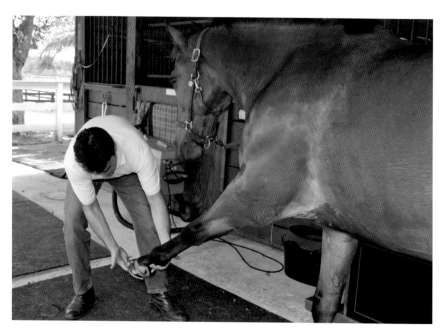

*4.2  Foreleg Forward Deep Stretch*

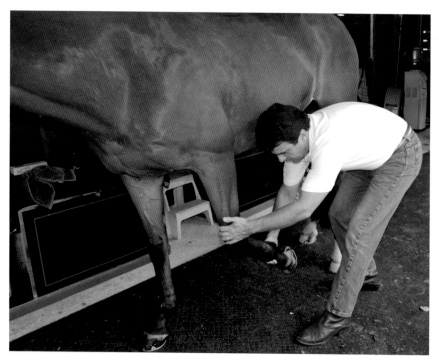

*4.3  Foreleg Backward Easy Stretch*

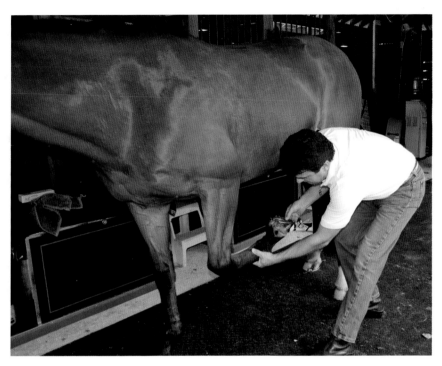

*4.4  Foreleg Backward Deep Stretch*

## THE SHOULDER ROTATION

The following movement will help loosen the deep muscles such as the pectoralis group, the serratus ventralis cervices and thoracis, the sub-scapularis, and the intercostal fascia, and will also relax the ligaments of the shoulder girdle structure.

Slide one hand between the chest and the forearm, and with your other hand gently grab the lower foreleg above the hoof as shown in figure 4.5. Start a circular movement moving the leg inward, then forward, outward, and back. Repeat several times (three to five times), and then reverse the movement moving the leg outward, then forward, inward, and back. Avoid excessive pressure at the shoulder joint.

Because of the nature of this particular stretch, the horse might take a little time to relax into it. Be patient, praise the horse as you comfort him. After several circles on either side, when you feel the horse is loosening into the movement, bring the leg out, as shown in figure 4.6 to stretch the entire shoulder muscle girdle.

## THE HIND LEG STRETCHES

There are three hind leg stretches: the forward stretch, the backward stretch, and the hind leg transverse stretch. Pay attention and make mental notes for each stretch, so when you stretch the opposite hind leg you

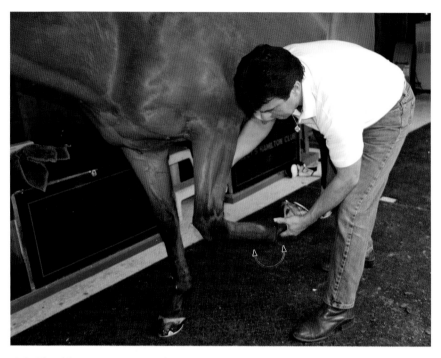

*4.5  Shoulder Rotation Stretch*

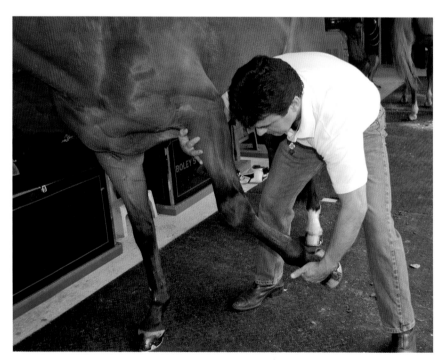

*4.6  Shoulder Side Stretch*

can compare and appreciate if both are even or not. If not, you will know which leg is more restricted, and in which way.

## The Forward Stretch

This protraction movement, also known as the hamstring stretch, will stretch the muscles involved in the retraction of the hind leg. With one hand, pick up the hoof. Position your other hand below and behind the hock joint, and gently move the leg forward in its natural line of movement. While the leg is forward you may consider moving it a little inward, as shown in figure 4.7. This is a good stretch for the muscles of the hip and thighs, the tensor fascia latae, the gluteals, and the hamstring muscles (the semi-tendinosus, the semi-membranosus, and the biceps femoris).

Once the horse is comfortable in the stretch, you can consider extending the hoof, as shown in figure 4.8. This will deepen the stretch over the flexor tendons and the suspensory ligaments, as well as the other various ligaments and joints of the hind leg. Be gentle and cautious.

## The Backward Stretch

This retraction movement will stretch the muscles involved in the flexion of the hip and of the leg. With one hand pick up the hoof and place your other hand in front of the canon bone. Bring the leg back through its natural range until you feel the stretch as shown in figure 4.9.

*4.7* ***Hind Leg Forward Easy Stretch***

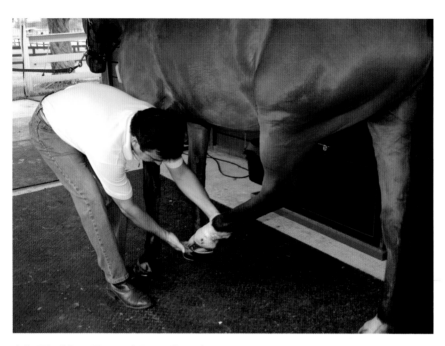

*4.8  Hind Leg Forward Deep Stretch*

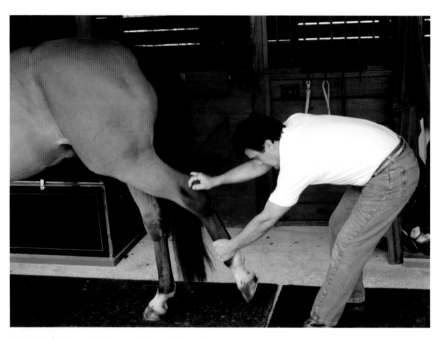

*4.9  Hind Leg Backward Easy Stretch*

Once the horse is comfortable in the stretch, you can consider flexing the hoof to deepen the stretch over the extensor tendons, as shown in figure 4.10. Be gentle and cautious. This is a good stretch for the following muscles: the iliacus, the sartorius, the tensor fascia latae, the quadriceps femoris, the extensor, and the abdominal muscles.

### The Hind Leg Transverse Stretch

This is another movement to stretch the quadriceps femoris muscle of the hind leg and the TFL (tensor fascia latae muscle).

Grasp the rear leg above the hoof on the opposite side of the horse, and bring the leg under the belly and slightly toward the opposite front hoof, as shown in figure 4.11. Be aware of the torque you will produce on the hock and the stifle joint by stretching this way. Do not apply too much pressure. Be gentle, paying attention to your horse's comfort.

## THE BACK MUSCLES STRETCHES

There is no particular stretching movement for the back muscles. But by reflex, you can affect these muscles if you press your thumb into the belly region, right over the attachment tendon of the pectoralis minor profondus muscle on the sternum bone, as shown in figure 4.12. This will cause the horse to tuck up, thereby rounding his back and stretching these muscles: longissimus dorsi, iliocostalis, and spinalis dorsi. Tickling the belly will also cause the same reflex. This is one of the easiest stretches.

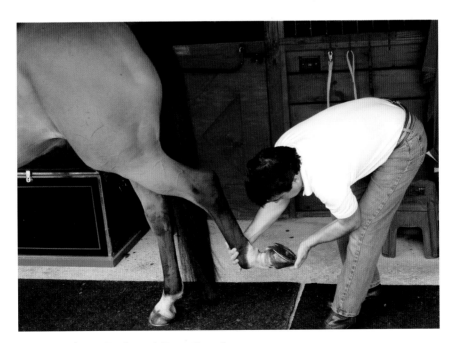

**4.10  Hind Leg Backward Deep Stretch**

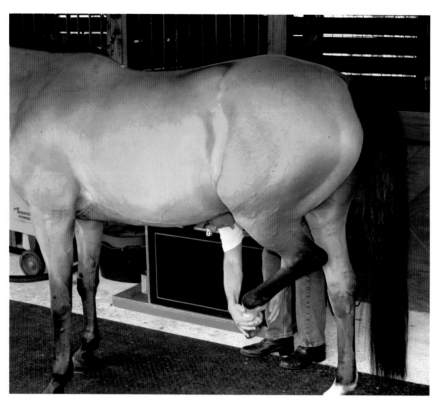

*4.11 Hind Leg Transverse Stretch*

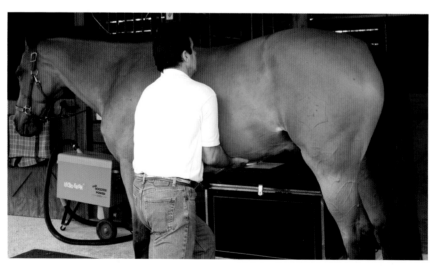

*4.12 Back Muscle Stretch from the Pectorals*

Another way to affect these muscles is to stimulate the sacrum area along its edges with some thumb point pressure moves, as shown in figure 4.13. This will cause a reflex action in the abdominal muscles, which will result in an arching of the back structure and a stretching of the back muscles.

## THE TAIL STRETCH

Stretching the tail is a great way to produce a feeling of deep relaxation in your horse. This stretch is a major part of the relaxation massage routine (see chapter 3, figures 3.5 through 3.9). When approaching the rear, use gentle strokings along the tailbone and down the buttocks before picking up the tail with your right hand. Leave your other hand on the sacrum. Take hold of the tail a few inches from its base and gently move it in a circle starting clockwise, two or three times. Repeat in the counterclockwise direction two or three times. During these movements, take note of any restriction found in moving the tail to either side.

Then start stretching the tail by bringing it upward, as shown in figure 4.14. This will stretch the tail depressor muscles (the sacrocaudalis ventralis muscle, one on each side).

Next, bring the tail into a question mark position, as shown in figure 4.15. Use your left hand to help stretch the tail into a question mark. Hold it in that stretch for five seconds and release. This will stretch the tail levator muscles (the sacrocaudalis dorsalis muscle, one on each side).

At this point, move to the back of the horse and very gently pull on the tail, as shown in figure 4.16. Apply 1 to 2 pounds of pressure

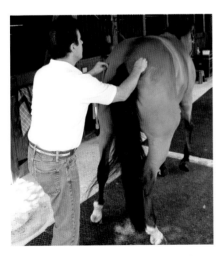

**4.13  Back Muscle Stretch from the Hinds**

**4.14  Raising the Tail Stretch**

*4.15* **Question Mark Stretch**          *4.16* **Tail Stretch**

maximum. Use your common sense and don't pull to the point of discomfort. Hold this stretch for approximately one minute, unless the horse shows discomfort. Usually the horse, feeling good, responds positively by pulling against your traction or lowering its head. This will stretch both the tail levator and depressor muscles as well as the deep ligaments that attach the tail to the sacrum.

To further the benefit of this stretch, perform some light muscle squeezing movements. While you keep stretching the tail with the left hand, use the thumb and fingers of your right hand to gently squeeze each vertebra from the base of the tail down. Reverse hands if that is more suitable to you. Make note of the tail's flexibility, looking for sore spots and possible inflammation. Release the stretch progressively and then stroke the hindquarters and sacrum area for a few seconds.

## NECK STRETCHES

These neck stretches will affect all aspects of the neck's muscles. You can do all stretches using an incentive such as a piece of horse biscuit. This makes the work much, much easier. Pay attention and make mental notes for each stretch, so that when you stretch the opposite side you can compare and appreciate whether both sides are even. If not, you will know which one is more restricted, and in what way.

### Lateral Stretch

Allow the horse to sniff the "incentive" and guide it toward his point of shoulder, as shown in figure 4.17. This movement will mostly stretch the upper aspect of the neck's extensor and flexor muscles on the opposite side.

You can increase the lateral stretch to the lower aspect of the neck by asking your horse to stretch further toward the point of the hip, as shown in figure 4.18. This movement will further stretch the lower aspect of the neck's extensor and flexor muscles on the opposite side.

Next, bring the "incentive" down at a midway point between the limbs and down at the level of the knee, as shown in figure 4.19.

Always talk softly to your animal as you get into the development of the stretches. Do both the right and left sides.

### Neck Flexion Stretch

Still using an incentive, guide your horse's head down between his legs, as shown in figure 4.20. In performing this particular stretch, you can add a variation: as you bring the head down, move his head either to the right or to the left. The extensor muscles will thus be thoroughly stretched.

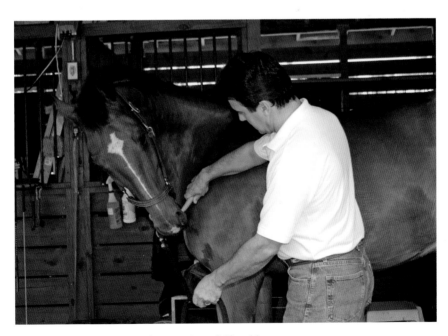

**4.17 *Lateral Neck Stretch to Point of Shoulder***

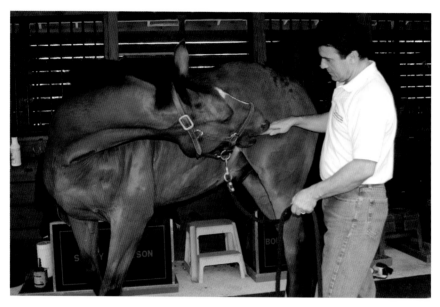

*4.18  Lateral Neck Stretch to Point of Hip*

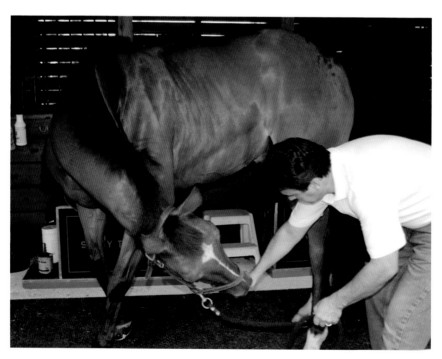

*4.19  Lateral Neck Stretch, Midway*

*4.20 Neck Flexion Stretch*

## Neck Extension Stretch

As with the other neck stretches, use an incentive to guide your horse's head upward and out as far as it can go, as shown in figure 4.21. This movement will stretch the neck's flexor muscles.

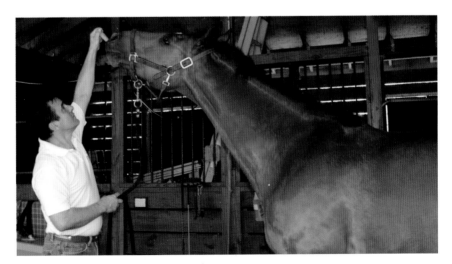

*4.21 Neck Extension Stretch*

## SUMMARY

Stretching exercises during your prepurchase evaluation will reveal a lot of information, not only about the horse's ability to be handled, but also about the flexibility and symmetry of his body parts. Restrictions seen during a stretch can be revealing of a horse's muscular tension, ligament soreness, or discomfort from a bony misalignment.

When you own a horse, stretching exercises are great, of course, since they will contribute to his overall flexibility and fitness. Also, the reaction of your horse to the stretch is a great source of feedback on how he carries himself. You should include stretching in your exercise program. Practice stretching your horse in the safe way presented here to become proficient at it.

# 5

## ANATOMICAL REVIEW

**T**his chapter presents a review of the important anatomical points of the equine musculoskeletal system needed in order to carry out your palpation evaluation efficiently. However, an in-depth anatomical description of the equine musculoskeletal system is beyond the scope of this book. For more in-depth information, please consult a veterinary anatomy atlas of the horse.

As you learn more about your horse's anatomy, become familiar with all the structures. Please take the time to palpate the bony landmarks such as the wings of the Atlas vertebrae right behind the head, the spinous processes of the thoracic vertebrae that form the withers, the ribs and the sternum, the junction of the last lumbar vertebrae and the sacrum, the sacrum and iliac junction, and the junction of the first coccygeal vertebrae to the sacrum. Feel the joints of the legs. Also, familiarize yourself with all the major muscle groups, with their origin and insertion tendons' locations.

For those interested in an in-depth study of equine kinesiology, the study of the muscles responsible for the horse's locomotion, and the various muscular and fascia compensation phenomenon, please refer to the book *Equine Muscular Compensation Study Manual* by this same author and available at the Massage Awareness Library (www.massageaware ness.com).

In this chapter, we will review the equine dentition, and the equine skeleton and muscle groups and their ligaments. We will also review trigger points and stress points, including a list of forty potential locations for stress point formation.

# DENTITION

Here is a quick review of the horse's dental structure. The adult horse usually has forty teeth distributed evenly between the upper and the lower jaws. So, on each side you'll find:

| Maxillary | 3 Molars | 3 Premolars | 1 Canine | 3 Incisors |
| Mandible | 3 Molars | 3 Premolars | 1 Canine | 3 Incisors |

This makes a total of twelve incisors, four canines, twelve premolars, and twelve molars. Usually the four canines are absent with mares, bringing the number of teeth to thirty-six. The incisors are positioned in an archlike way on each jaw. They are respectively named:

The center incisors: the two center teeth

The lateral incisors: between the center and the corner incisors

The corner incisors: the two on the edges

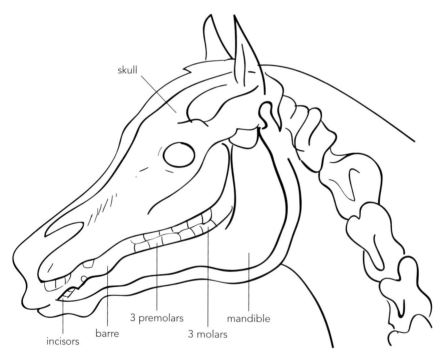

*5.1 Equine Teeth*

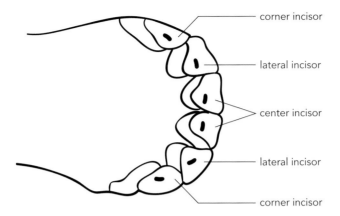

corner incisor

lateral incisor

center incisor

lateral incisor

corner incisor

*5.2  Equine Incisors Arch*

The smoothness of mastication and the health of the TMJ are dependent on the good float of the mandible over the maxilla. At the level of the first premolar all the way to the last molar, the shape of the mandible interacts with the maxillary in a harmonious curve, known as the curve of Spee. When uneven teeth develop, which eventually become "hooks," they will interfere with the smooth functioning of the mastication apparatus.

Also, the angle formed between the upper molars that sag over the lower molars is supposed to be a descending angle of 21 degrees, with a medial to lateral slant, as well as a dorsal to ventral slant. This is known as the curve of Wilson.

When both curves, the curve of Spee and the curve of Wilson, are working harmoniously, the ideal occlusion is reached for optimal mastication, and good health of the TMJs is maintained.

More extensive information on equine dentistry is beyond the scope of this book. Please refer to professional literature for further details.

## THE SKELETON

The equine skeleton is divided in two parts, the *axial skeleton* and the *appendicular skeleton*, the limbs. Let us first focus on the axial skeleton since it is the "anchor" to which all major muscle groups attach.

*5.3  Curve of Spee*

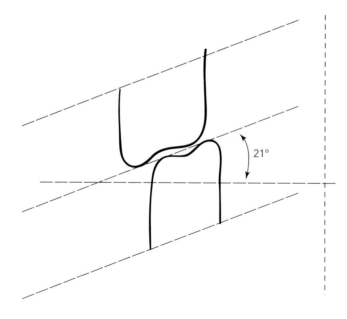

21°

*5.4  Curve of Wilson*

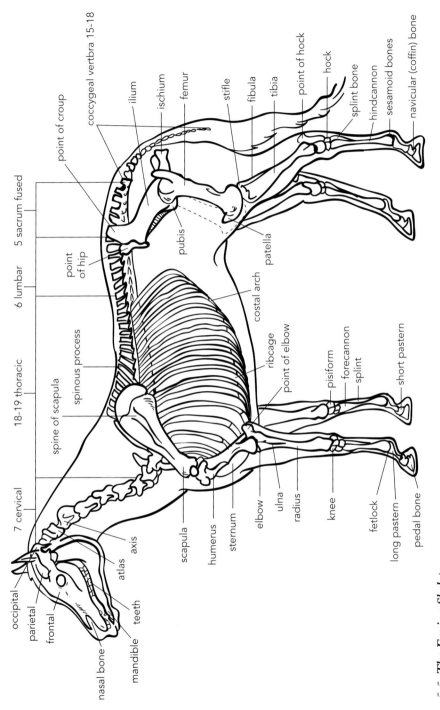

*5.5  The Equine Skeleton*

## THE AXIAL SKELETON

The axial skeleton includes the skull, the entire vertebral column, and the rib cage. The skull is the seat of the central nervous system (brain), the vertebral column contains the spine (cauda equina), and the rib cage protects the heart and lungs. Besides protecting the spinal cord, the vertebral column provides a strong structure made up of a series of vertebrae separated by joints, reinforced by ligaments and muscles. This solid structure offers anchoring for muscle groups, as well as resisting the downward effect of gravity. The vertebral column has some flexibility in four directions: flexion, extension, lateral bending, and rotation, which are mostly seen in the cervical (neck) and caudal (tail) section of the column.

From the skull to the end of the tail the spine is a chainlike arrangement of about fifty-four medium-size irregular bones called vertebrae in which runs the spinal cord. The vertebral column is divided in five parts: the cervical part with seven vertebrae, the thoracic part with eighteen vertebrae, the lumbar part with six vertebrae, the sacral part with five fused vertebrae, and finally the coccygeal part with usually eighteen vertebrae on average. The formula C7-T18-L6-S5-Cd18 is an easy way to remember the composition of the spine.

Most vertebrae are movable and articulate while some are naturally fused, like the five sacral vertebrae that form the sacrum. Otherwise vertebrae articulate with each other by means of a series of synovial joints between articular processes, and by fibrous joints between the vertebral bodies.

The rib cage attaches to the thoracic section (T1–T18) of the vertebral column. Eighteen pairs of ribs come to anchor from T1 to T18. Dorsally, the head of the ribs articulate with the *costal foveae* of two contiguous thoracic vertebrae and the intervening fibrocartilage. The dorsal costotransversal ligaments help anchor the head of the ribs to the vertebral column. Ventrally, the ribs meet to form the sternum.

*5.6 The Axial Skeleton*

   skull, cervical 7, thoracic 18, lumbar 6, sacrum 5, tail 18

## THE APPENDICULAR SKELETON

The appendicular skeleton includes the forelimb and the hind limb. They provide the structure for locomotion of the axial skeleton. The limbs are made up of a series of bones linked by joints, reinforced by ligaments and muscles, as shown in figure 5.7. The limbs move in four directions: protraction, retraction, adduction, and abduction.

## SPINAL SUBLUXATION

The vertebral column is a string of flexible, movable bones and discs that protect the vulnerable spinal cords and nerve roots. Unfortunately, for various reasons ranging from trauma to bad falls, the bones of the spine can be pushed out of alignment, causing pressure on the nerve root and resulting in referred pain into the body. This condition is referred to as a *subluxation*. When movement between two or more vertebrae is restricted, the overall flexibility of the spine will be affected. The horse will display stiffness and resistance to bending or to executing certain maneuvers.

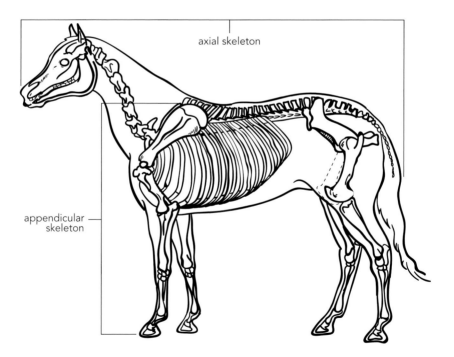

*5.7  The Appendicular Skeleton: Forelimb and Hind Limb*

During your massage palpation evaluation, pay attention to your four T's (see chapter 1). With a subluxation, the muscle groups attaching in the direct area will be affected and will display stronger muscle tension, even spasms, trigger points, and sometimes inflammation symptoms, as a result of the discomfort or pain produced by such vertebral misalignment. More often than not, a primary subluxation in the spine may cause the horse to compensate. This will trigger the formation of extra muscular tension, extra stress points, and trigger points. By trying to avoid the painful movement, the horse will shift his weight distribution. This compensation often causes a secondary subluxation to develop in other areas of the spine.

Keep in mind that the symptoms of a subluxation depend on its severity; therefore symptoms can vary from a mild pain discomfort to severe pain upon touch or movement. If the pain is minimal, the horse might just display some discomfort during riding with a shorter stride or lateral bend, upon saddling (girthing up), or even just some restlessness when standing. Stiffness or movement, lack of coordination, or gait abnormality are seen when vertebra are subluxated.

If the pain is strong the horse will be sensitive to touch, will pin his ears back, will resist commands or collected or lateral movement, will refuse jumping when asked, and eventually will develop unusual behavior pattern such as throwing his neck up or stretching it out. Such soreness is often seen as the horse displays facial expressions of pain. In such instances, please contact your veterinary chiropractor immediately.

## LIGAMENTS AND JOINTS OF THE HORSE

Ligaments are tough fibrous bands of connective tissue, connecting one bone to another to protect the joint. Their functions are to support the joint(s) and restrict their range of motion. During your massage palpation evaluation you will thoroughly check all leg joint and their ligaments.

If a ligament is inflamed, the soreness response of the horse will be revealing. Pay attention to your four T's. Most often a ligament is partially ruptured. In that case, the broken fibers usually retract onto themselves. So you might feel a little bump on both sides of the joint protected by that particular ligament. When a ligament is completely ruptured, the horse is very lame and requires surgery. Most likely you wouldn't be performing a prepurchase massage evaluation palpation at such time.

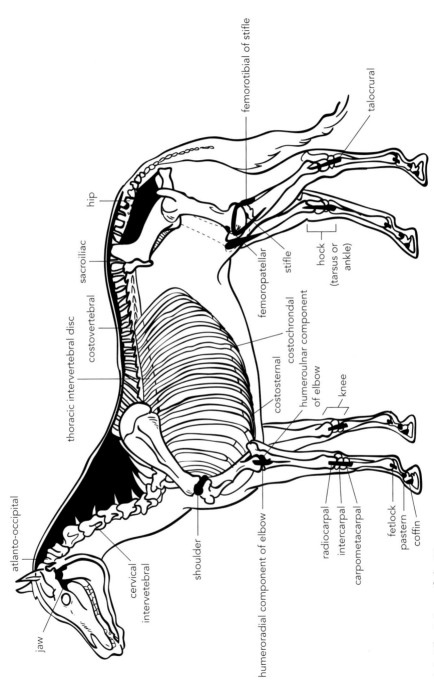

5.8 *The Joints of the Horse*

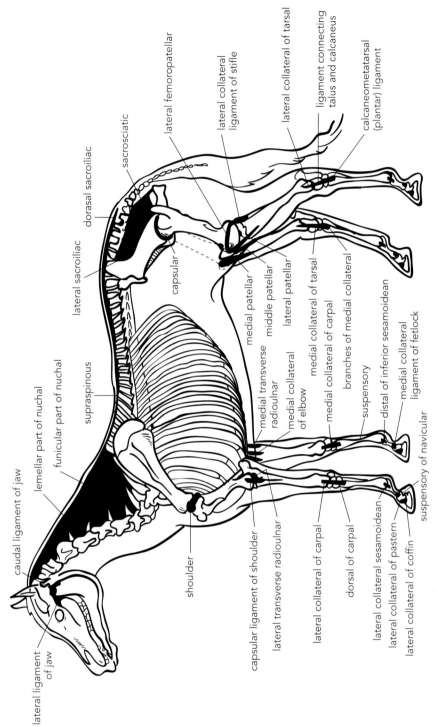

5.9 *The Ligaments of the Horse*

# THE EQUINE MUSCULAR SYSTEM

The muscular system provides the power and means to move the bony frame. In equine massage, we are concerned with the more than seven hundred skeletal muscles that are responsible for movement in the horse. Tight muscles are revealing of underlying condition. Train your eyes to quickly evaluate the size and tone of the various muscle groups on both sides of the horse. Then concentrate your palpation evaluation on the hypertonic muscles. Pay attention to your four T's (see chapter 1).

## MUSCLES

A muscle is made up of a fleshy part and two tendon attachments. The muscle belly, or fleshy part, is the part that contracts in response to a nervous command. During contraction, the muscle fibers basically fold on themselves, which shortens them and results in muscle movement. The muscle belly is made up of many muscle fibers arranged in bundles with each bundle wrapped in connective tissue (fascia), as shown in figure 5.10. The fascia covers, supports, and separates each individual muscle bundle and the whole muscle itself. This arrangement allows for greater support, strength, and flexibility in the movement between each of the muscle groups.

### Skeletal Muscles

Muscles come in all shapes and sizes. Some are small and some large, some are thin and some are bulky. Look at the muscle charts to note the variety of shapes in the horse's muscle structure.

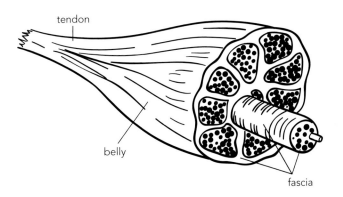

*5.10 Cross Section of a Skeletal Muscle*

Muscles act together to give the horse its grace and power. Skeletal muscles are highly elastic and have strong contractile power. A heavily exercised muscle will often develop a light inflammation within its fibers. This is a normal process that promotes formation of new muscle fibers. It is often seen during early phases of training, or in growing horses. But it is important to keep any inflammation under control to avoid the formation of scar tissue.

As a result of heavy exercise, a stress point may develop close to the origin tendon of the muscle. A stress point is a small spasm in the muscle fiber. Another side effect of an intense training and exercise program is the formation of trigger points. A trigger point is a combination of lactic acid buildup and motor nerve ending irritation mostly found in the fleshy part (belly) of the muscle. Trigger points can be found in any muscle of the body. Study all the muscle charts and learn about all aspects of the horse's body. Understanding the interrelation of all the components of the musculoskeletal system will contribute greatly to your expertise in evaluating a horse's musculoskeletal structure.

## TENDONS

The tendon is the muscle part that attaches to the bone. The tendon is made up of connective tissue, a dense, white fibrous tissue, much like that of a ligament. The origin tendon is the tendon that attaches the muscle to the least-movable bone, whereas the insertion tendon is the tendon that attaches the muscle to the movable bone, so that on contraction the insertion is brought closer to the origin. Tendons attach to the periosteum of the bone; the fibers of the tendon blend with the periosteum fibers because of their similar collagen makeup. Tendons can be fairly short or quite long, as seen on some of the flexor and extensor muscles of the lower legs. Usually tendons are rounded, but they can be flattened like the tendons attached along the spine, or like the aponeurosis tendon of the external abdominal oblique muscle.

Because of their high-tensile strength, tendons can endure an enormous amount of tension, usually more than the muscle itself can produce; consequently, tendons do not rupture easily. They are not as elastic as muscle fibers, but they are more elastic than ligament fibers.

Tendons can "stress up" after heavy exercise, meaning that they can stay contracted. Gentle massage and stretching will loosen residual tension.

Inflamed tendons are at great risk of being strained or overstretched. Many leg muscles have long tendons that run down the legs, over the joints. Sheaths, or tendon bursa, protect these tendons. Chronic irritation of the sheath can result in excess fluid production and soft swellings.

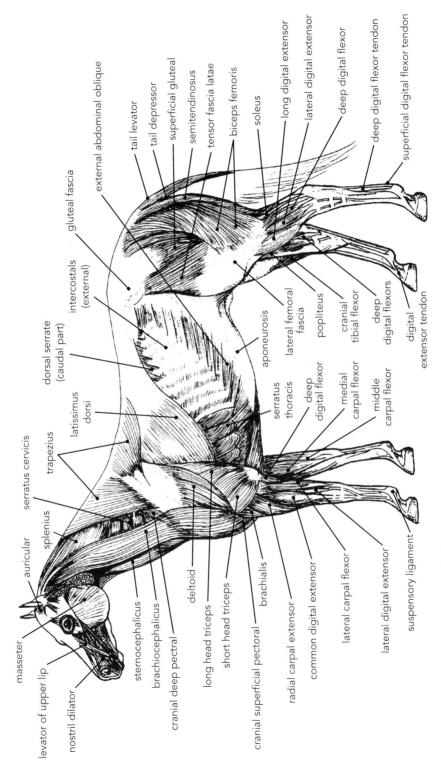

*5.11 Muscles of the Horse, Superficial Layer*

masseter
auricular
levator of upper lip
nostril dilator
serratus cervicis
splenius
trapezius
latissimus dorsi
dorsal serrate (caudal part)
intercostals (external)
gluteal fascia
external abdominal oblique
tail levator
tail depressor
superficial gluteal
semitendinosus
tensor fascia latae
biceps femoris
soleus
long digital extensor
lateral digital extensor
deep digital flexor
deep digital flexor tendon
superficial digital flexor tendon

sternocephalicus
brachiocephalicus
cranial deep pectral
deltoid
long head triceps
short head triceps
cranial superficial pectoral
brachialis
radial carpal extensor
common digital extensor
lateral carpal flexor
lateral digital extensor
suspensory ligament
serratus thoracis
deep digital flexor
medial carpal flexor
middle carpal flexor
aponeurosis
lateral femoral fascia
popliteus
cranial tibial flexor
deep digital flexors
digital extensor tendon

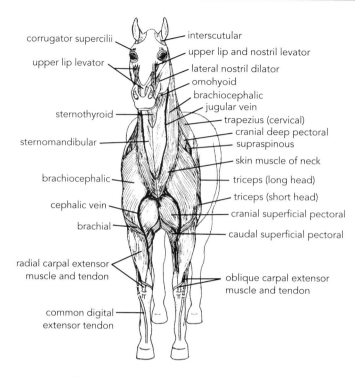

corrugator supercilii
upper lip levator
sternothyroid
sternomandibular
brachiocephalic
cephalic vein
brachial
radial carpal extensor
muscle and tendon
common digital
extensor tendon

interscutular
upper lip and nostril levator
lateral nostril dilator
omohyoid
brachiocephalic
jugular vein
trapezius (cervical)
cranial deep pectoral
supraspinous
skin muscle of neck
triceps (long head)
triceps (short head)
cranial superficial pectoral
caudal superficial pectoral
oblique carpal extensor
muscle and tendon

*5.12  Muscles of the Horse, Anterior (Front) View*

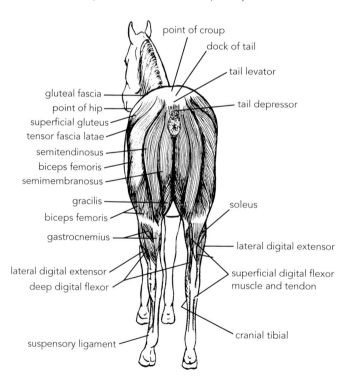

point of croup
dock of tail
tail levator
gluteal fascia
point of hip
superficial gluteus
tensor fascia latae
semitendinosus
biceps femoris
semimembranosus
gracilis
biceps femoris
gastrocnemius
lateral digital extensor
deep digital flexor
suspensory ligament

tail depressor
soleus
lateral digital extensor
superficial digital flexor
muscle and tendon
cranial tibial

*5.13  Muscles of the Horse, Posterior (Rear) View*

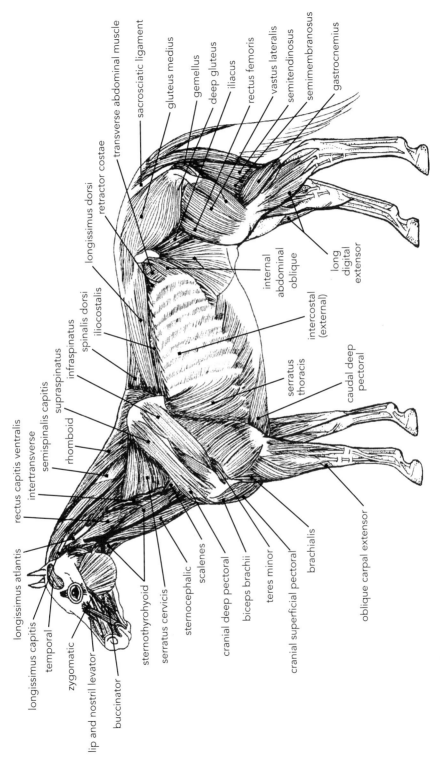

*5.14 Muscles of the Horse, Deeper Layer*

transverse abdominal muscle
sacrosciatic ligament
gluteus medius
gemellus
deep gluteus
iliacus
rectus femoris
vastus lateralis
semitendinosus
semimembranosus
gastrocnemius

retractor costae
longissimus dorsi

internal abdominal oblique

long digital extensor

intercostal (external)

spinalis dorsi
iliocostalis
supraspinatus
infraspinatus
semispinalis capitis
intertransverse
rhomboid

serratus thoracis

caudal deep pectoral

rectus capitis ventralis
longissimus atlantis
longissimus capitis
temporal
zygomatic
lip and nostril levator
buccinator
sternothyrohyoid
serratus cervicis
sternocephalic
scalenes
cranial deep pectoral
biceps brachii
teres minor
cranial superficial pectoral
brachialis

oblique carpal extensor

# TRIGGER POINTS

A trigger point forms primarily as the result of toxin buildup (mostly lactic acid, the resulting by-product from burning glycogen, the main energy source for muscles, and oxygen). Because of the toxicity in the fibers, an irritation of the local motor nerve endings develops. The term *trigger point* originates in the fact that pressure applied to that particular point would send a pain referral to other body parts. The presence and association of the nerve endings throughout the muscle groups mostly cause this referred pain.

A trigger point is usually found in the belly part of a muscle. Depending on your horse's level and type of activity, trigger points can form in several muscles anywhere in the body. This condition occurs mostly in response to muscle tension (overuse) or nervous stress; it can sometimes be due to a lack of activity (sluggish circulation). The hyper-tonicity or hypotonicity of the muscle fibers causes a decrease in blood circulation as well as a decrease in oxygen, resulting in a buildup of toxins. The increase in toxin in one particular area will trigger a nerve ending irritation.

Muscular tension (hypertonocity) is mostly due to overwork and not enough time spent on cooling down, stretching, or resting. Keep in mind that excess fatigue, nervous stress, restlessness, or boredom can also trigger the same muscular tension.

When the referred pain is of weak intensity, it is termed a *silent trigger point,* whereas one that sends strong sensations and is very sensitive to the touch is referred to as an *active trigger point.* Frequently, trigger points are found within symptom referral areas. Occasionally, one trigger point will have more than one referral area; these are called spillover areas.

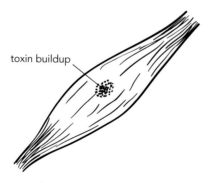

toxin buildup

*5.15 Schematic Diagram of a Trigger Point*

Trigger points feel like small nodules but can occasionally appear as larger nodules; in any size, they are usually very tender. Trigger points give easily under pressure and release fairly quickly. Hot hydrotherapy application (a hot towel) over the specific area will contribute greatly to loosening the tissue fibers and boosting the circulation in the area.

## STRESS POINTS

Stress points are micro spasms involving only a few fibers out of a whole bundle of fibers. However, if untreated, these micro spasms can turn into full-blown muscle spasms.

A stress point feels like a spot of hardened, rigid tissue about the size of the end of your little finger or less. It does not move under the fingers, may be slightly swollen, and will feel tender to the horse when touched. If a stress point is not inflamed it is referred to as a *dormant* stress point. If a stress point is inflamed it is referred to as an *active* stress point, which will display more tenderness and will eventually produce heat and swelling. Many horses experience tight muscles, resulting in a reduced muscle action (shorter stride or lameness) due to stress point development within these muscles.

Stress points will most often develop at a muscle's origin tendon, which is the tendon that anchors the muscle to the stable, nonmovable body part during contraction. The origin tendon tends to be quite strong and of good size because it is the anchor attachment for the muscle, and therefore sustains great mechanical strain. The other tendon, the insertion tendon, attaches the muscle to the movable part.

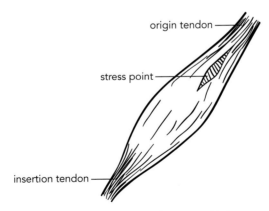

*5.16 Schematic Diagram of a Stress Point*

Stress points form as a result of great mechanical stress that causes microtearing of the muscle fibers. Heavy training, repetitive actions, weight overload, and strenuous effort are all examples of great mechanical stress. Stress points can also develop as a response to direct trauma such as a bump or a fall, or as a result of overstretching. After an injury and during the recovery stage, the muscular compensation developing in the rest of a horse's body will trigger formation of other stress points within the compensatory muscles. For example, a horse with a sore knee will develop compensatory stress points in the shoulder muscles as well as in the muscle attaching the scapula to the rest of the body. If really lame, the horse will switch his weight onto the other legs to relieve pressure on the sore knee, causing a great deal of muscular strain on the other limbs and resulting in new stress point formation.

Stress points can be found anywhere in the muscular structure of the horse. Due to the nature of the horse's locomotor apparatus, there are some well-known areas of the skeleton and related specific muscles where stress points are usually found. A list of forty of the most common stress point locations seen with the equine athlete is shown on pages 59 to 61.

## SUMMARY

A solid understanding of the anatomical structures of your horse will contribute greatly to the development of your palpation skills for the application of the PEP. If you are interested in learning your horse muscles, try drawing the skeleton and the various muscle groups; this will assist you in memorizing their actual location.

This knowledge of the structures, combined with your palpation skills, will allow you to flow harmoniously and confidently from one body part to another during your sessions with your horse of choice.

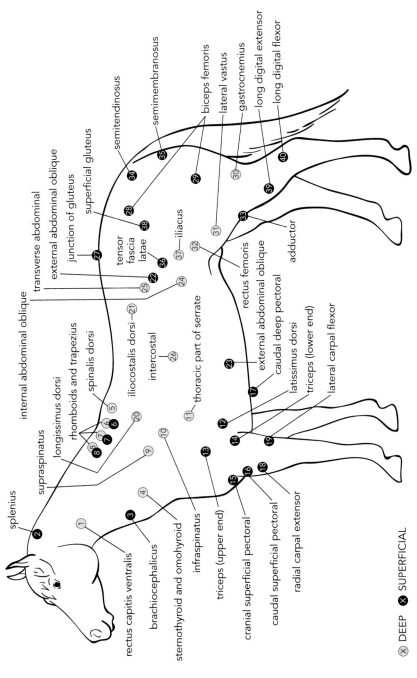

splenius

supraspinatus

longissimus dorsi

rhomboids and trapezius

spinalis dorsi

internal abdominal oblique

transverse abdominal

external abdominal oblique

junction of gluteus

superficial gluteus

semitendinosus

semimembranosus

biceps femoris

lateral vastus

gastrocnemius

long digital extensor

long digital flexor

tensor fascia latae

iliacus

iliocostalis dorsi

intercostal

thoracic part of serrate

rectus femoris

external abdominal oblique

caudal deep pectoral

adductor

latissimus dorsi

triceps (lower end)

lateral carpal flexor

rectus capitis ventralis

brachiocephalicus

sternothyroid and omohyroid

infraspinatus

triceps (upper end)

cranial superficial pectoral

caudal superficial pectoral

radial carpal extensor

⊗ DEEP    ⊗ SUPERFICIAL

*5.17 Equine Stress Point, Side View Chart (MAInc. 1995)*

1. **Rectus Capitis Ventralis Muscle:** *Flexion and lateral flexion of the head*
2. **Splenius Muscle:** *Lateral flexion of the head*
3. **Brachiocephalicus Muscle:** *Sideways head and neck movement, lifts foreleg*
4. **Sternothyrohyoideus and Omohyoideus Muscles:** *Flexes neck to side, rotates head to opposite side*
5. **Spinalis Dorsi:** *Extends the back, lift ribs (inhalation)*
6. **Rhomboideus and Trapezius Muscles:** *Draws scapula upward, forward and backward (posterior aspect.)*
7. **Rhomboideus and Trapezius Muscles:** *Draws scapula upward, forward, and backward (middle aspect).*
8. **Rhomboideus and Trapezius Muscles:** *Draws scapula upward, forward, and backward (anterior aspect).*
9. **Supraspinatus Muscle:** *Extension of shoulder joint, prevents dislocation*
10. **Infraspinatus Muscle:** *Abduction, rotation of shoulder joint, prevents dislocation*
11. **Serratus Ventralis Thoracic Muscle:** *Draws scapula backward, draws trunk upward*
12. **Latissimus Dorsi Muscle:** *Draws leg backward*
13. **Triceps Muscle (Proximal End):** *Flexes shoulder joint*
14. **Triceps Muscle (Distal End):** *Extends and locks elbow joint*
15. **Cranial Superficial Pectoral Muscle:** *Adducts foreleg during movement*
16. **Caudal Superficial Pectoral Muscle:** *Adducts foreleg during movement*
17. **Caudal Deep Pectoral Muscle:** *Adducts and draws foreleg backward*
18. **Radial Carpal Extensor Muscle:** *Extends hoof during movement*
19. **Lateral Carpal Flexor Muscle:** *Flexes hoof during movement*
20. **Longissimus Dorsi Muscle:** *Extends back and loins, lateral flexion*
21. **Iliocostalis Dorsi Muscle:** *Lateral flexion of trunk*
22. **External Abdominal Oblique Muscle (hip):** *Flexes trunk straight and laterally*
23. **External Abdominal Oblique Muscle (rib cage):** *Flexes trunk straight and laterally*
24. **Internal Abdominal Oblique Muscle (belly):** *Flexes trunk straight and laterally*
25. **Transversus Abdominus Muscle:** *Flexes trunk straight and laterally*
26. **Intercostal (10th Rib) Muscles:** *Flexes trunk straight and laterally*
27. **Junction of the Middle Gluteal and Longissimus Dorsi Muscles:** *Forward propulsion*
28. **Biceps Femoris Muscle:** *Extends and abducts hind leg, flexes stifle*
29. **Biceps Femoris Muscle (belly part):** *Flexes stifle*
30. **Gastrocnemius Muscle:** *Extends of hock, flexes stifle*
31. **Vastus Lateralis Muscle:** *Flexes hip/femur*
32. **Rectus Femoris Muscle (by stifle):** *Flexes hip/femur*
33. **Adductor Muscles (femur insertion):** *Adducts hind leg*
34. **Semitendinosus Muscle:** *Extends hip, flexes stifle, medial rotation of leg*
35. **Semimembranosus Muscle:** *Extends hip, flexes stifle*
36. **Tensor Fasciae Latae Muscle:** *Flexes hip, extends stifle*
37. **Iliacus Muscle:** *Flexes hip, rotates thigh outward*
38. **Superficial Gluteal Muscle:** *Extends hip, rotates thigh outward*
39. **Long Digital Extensor Muscle:** *Extends hoof*
40. **Long Digital Flexor Muscle:** *Flexes hoof*

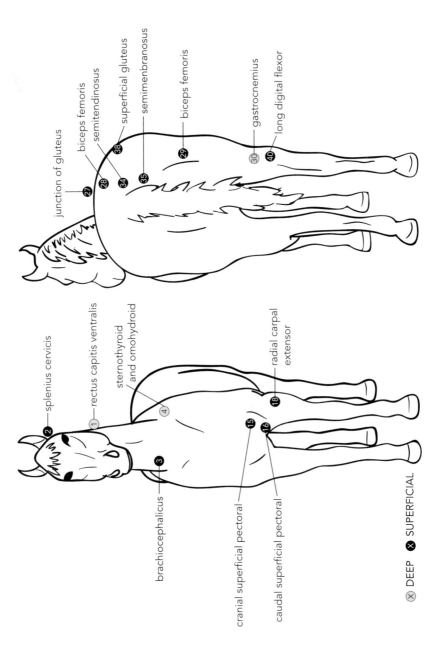

junction of gluteus
biceps femoris
semitendinosus
superficial gluteus
semimenbranosus
biceps femoris
gastrocnemius
long digital flexor

27
28
34
38
35
29
30
40

splenius cervicis
rectus capitis ventralis
sternothyroid and omohydroid
radial carpal extensor
brachiocephalicus
cranial superficial pectoral
caudal superficial pectoral

2
1
4
18
3
15
16

⊗ DEEP  ⊗ SUPERFICIAL

5.18 *Equine Stress Point, Front and Hind View Chart*

# 6

## CONFORMATION AND STANCES EVALUATION

Having a good understanding of equine conformation and of the various horse stances is a great advantage when evaluating your horse, and especially when dealing with a new horse. Such an in-depth study of equine conformation for each breed and discipline is beyond the scope of this book, so please refer to specialized literature for this information. The following guidelines will help you gain a solid knowledge of the various conformations and stances seen with horses. This will help you with the visual portion of your evaluation.

When observing a horse's conformation, it is best to position the horse on an even, flat surface. Before you start, have the horse stand square, meaning with his two rear pasterns vertical from the hocks to the fetlocks.

## CONFORMATION

Not all horses have the same physical ability to do everything that is asked of them. Some types of conformation are structurally better suited to perform in certain disciplines, and some breeds are better suited to them as well. For example, the breeds listed below excel in specific sports or disciplines:

- ❖ Thoroughbreds: dressage, hunter, jumper, eventing, racing
- ❖ Warmbloods: dressage, hunter, jumper, eventing
- ❖ Arabians: show under saddle, endurance
- ❖ Saddlebreds: show under saddle, driving
- ❖ Quarter Horses: Western performance, hunter, jumper, racing
- ❖ Ponies: hunter, jumper, driving, mounted games
- ❖ Appaloosas and Paints: endurance, eventing, and Western performance

Each discipline or sport demands the best of the horse's physical capabilities, and of course, some classes demand more than others. The competitive nature of horse sports makes it necessary for the animal to use his entire body at once. Specific activities trigger the development of particular stress sites, particularly when the horse's conformation is not ideal for the work undertaken. Thus, stress points can develop at any time and anywhere in the body. For more on stress point locations on the horse, see chapter 20.

A horse with a compact and uphill build is definitely an advantage to develop an elastic gait, to bend the joints, and to work the horse with impulsion and power. On the other end, faulty conformation can result in a variety of problems:

- ❖ A longer-backed horse may be prone to developing more stress points than a shorter-backed horse.
- ❖ A horse with a long cannon bone will tend to be more prone to tendon and ligament problems than a horse with a shorter cannon bone and proportionally shorter tendons and ligaments.
- ❖ A neck too long, too short, or set too high can have difficulty bending and achieving good contact at the bit. Also, poor dentition, or TMJ, can lead to poor contact.
- ❖ Weak hindquarters can cause the problem of self-carriage from behind, leading to a contact problem with the rider's hand.

## FRONT-LEG CONFORMATION

A good conformation in the front end is important, since it is the steering apparatus of the horse. Keep your personal goals in mind when purchasing a horse. It will strongly influence how you may interpret your findings during your evaluation.

### When Standing in Front of the Horse

An ideal structure can be identified by a theoretical plumb line that travels downward from a point at the center of the scapulo-humeral joint (shoulder joint), dividing the limb equally through the elbow, knee, and fetlock, and ending at a point on the center of the hoof, as shown in figure 6.1.

### Base Narrow
If the plumb line ends laterally (on the outside) to the hoof, it means the leg is inclined inward, indicating that the horse will bear more weight on the outside of his leg, stressing the lateral aspect of the leg's musculoskeletal and fascia structures. There will also be more compression on the medial aspect of the limb, also stressing the medial aspect of the leg musculoskeletal and fascia structures. When both legs show that characteristic, it is referred to as *base narrow*.

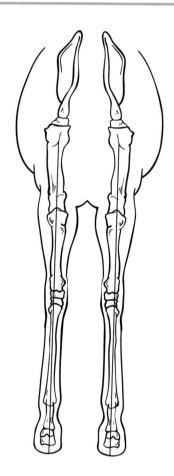

*6.1 Front Leg Ideal Cranial Plumb Line*

### Base Narrow, Toe-in

If the hoof is *toe-in*, it will create that much more stress, directly proportional to the degree of abnormality, over the lateral aspect of the entire limb. The collateral ligaments of each joint of the foreleg would be stressed. It could affect the shoulder girdle muscles.

### Base Narrow, Toe-out

If the hoof is *toe-out*, it will still cause much stress on the medial aspect of the leg, but this time more so onto the entire fetlock and phalanx, resulting in muscular and ligament tension over the metacarpal and digital areas.

### Knock-Knees

You might also see the knees deviated medially, a condition known as *knock-knees*. This reveals stress on both aspects of the knee joint: medially as the collateral ligaments are strained, and laterally as the concussion on the carpus is greater. Extra stress would be found over the flexor muscle and possibly in the pectoral muscles.

### Bowleg

You might also see the knees deviated laterally, a condition known as *bowleg*. This reveals stress on both aspects of the knee joint: medially as the concussion on the carpus bones is greater and laterally as the collateral ligaments are strained. Extra stress would also be found over the extensor muscle and possibly in the shoulder muscles.

### Base Wide

If that plumb line ends medially (on the inside) to the hoof, it means the leg is inclined outward indicating that the horse will bear more weight on the inside of his leg, stressing the medial aspect of the leg musculoskeletal structures. When both legs show that characteristic, it is referred to as *base wide*; this is often seen with narrow-chested horses.

### Base Wide, Toe-in

If the hoof is *toe-in*, it will accentuate the stress, directly proportional to the degree of abnormality, onto the lateral collateral ligaments of each joint of that leg.

### Base Wide, Toe-out

If the hoof is *toe-out*, stress will be more localized over the medial aspect of the leg, affecting the collateral ligaments of each joint of that leg.

## When Standing at the Side the Horse

An ideal conformation structure can be identified by a theoretical plumb line that should travel downward from the tuber spinae on the spine of the scapula, dividing the limb equally, through the fetlock and ending just behind the heel, as shown in figure 6.2.

### Over at the Knee

When standing properly, if the horse's knee appears to be forward, a condition referred to as *over at the knee*, suspect stress over both the flexor and extensor muscles and the suspensory ligament.

### Calf Knee

If the knee appears to be going back, a condition referred to as *calf knee*, suspect stress over the collateral and accessory ligaments and both the flexor and extensor muscles.

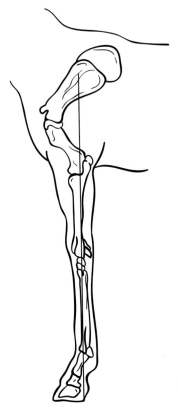

*6.2 **Front Leg Ideal Lateral Plumb Line***

## Standing-Under

If the limb is placed behind the theoretical plumb line, it is referred to as *standing-under*. If the limb is placed too far forward, it is referred to as *camped-under*. Both conditions will place undue stress on the entire leg structure, causing muscle tension in both the flexor and extensor muscles of the foreleg as well as in the collateral ligaments of its joints.

These guidelines will help you to quickly evaluate the forelegs of your horse, to understand what he is naturally showing you, and where you will find his musculoskeletal stress.

## HIND-LEG CONFORMATION

A good conformation in the rear end is important, since it is the power engine of the horse. As with the foreleg apparatus, keep your personal goals in mind when purchasing a horse. It will strongly influence how you may interpret your findings during your evaluation.

### When Standing Behind the Horse

An ideal conformation structure can be identified by a theoretical plumb line that should travel downward from the point of the tuber ischii, passing through the middle of the hock, the fetlock, and the hoof, as shown in figure 6.3.

### Base Narrow

If the plumb line ends laterally (on the outside) to the hoof, it means the leg is inclined inward, indicating that the horse will bear more weight on the outside of his leg, stressing primarily the lateral but also the medial aspect of the leg's musculoskeletal structures. When both legs show that characteristic, it is referred to as *base narrow*.

### Base Wide

On the other hand, if that plumb line ends medially (on the inside) to the hoof, it means the leg is inclined outward, indicating that the horse will bear more weight on the inside of his leg, stressing primarily the medial but also the lateral aspect of the leg musculoskeletal structures. When both legs show that characteristic, it is referred to as *base wide*.

### Cow-Hocked

The base wide condition described above, is often associated with a condition referred to as *cow-hocked,* where both hock joints accentuate a medial deviation. This combination puts a lot of stress on the medial aspect of the hock joints, resulting in bone spavin. This conformation will definitely cause a reduction in speed during locomotion.

### When Standing Beside, or Laterally to the Horse

An ideal conformation structure can be identified by a theoretical plumb line that should travel downward from the tip of the tuber ischii, touching the point of the hock, flowing parallel to the metatarsal (canon) and ending a couple inches behind the hoof, as shown in figure 6.4.

### Post-Legged

When the hind leg is positioned in front of that theoretical line, it is called *post-legged*. The term refers to a straight leg and is due to a lack of angle in the stifle and hock joints. This is revealing of stress on both the stifle and the hock joints. Typically, there will be some chronic muscular tension in the upper aspect of the hind leg with this condition.

### Camped Out Behind

If the theoretical line falls on the hoof or in front of the hoof, this is a condition referred to as *camped out behind*. This also reveals stress in the stifle, the hock, and the fetlock joints. Typically, muscular and fascia stress restrictions would be found over the lower back, upper thigh, and lower leg.

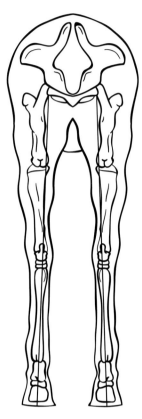

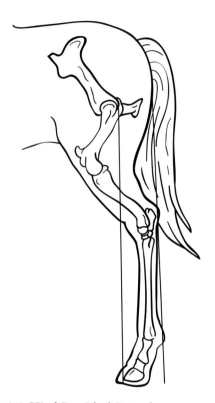

6.3 *Hind Leg Ideal Caudal*
    *Plumb Line*

6.4 *Hind Leg Ideal Lateral*
    *Plumb Line*

*Standing-Under*

If the theoretical line falls farther behind the hoof, this is referred to as *standing-under*. This condition reveals stress on both the stifle and the hock joints. Muscular and fascia stress would be found over the thigh and gaskin. If the angulation of the hock is excessive, it is referred to as *sickle hock* or *curby behind*. This condition will further stress the crural and tarsal fasciae as well as the plantar ligament.

How much is too much or not enough angulation? This depends on two major factors: breed and function. Again, presenting in-depth knowledge of equine conformation for each breed and discipline is beyond the scope of this book; please refer to specialized literature. Meanwhile, these guidelines will help you with your visual evaluation of any given horse.

# HORSE STANCES

Looking at the horse stance will help you further evaluate any areas of discomfort. This section helps you understand a horse's stance while at rest. The way he carries his head and the way he moves and positions his body, legs, and tail reveal a lot of precious information about his physical well-being. Keep in mind that a healthy horse takes different stances throughout the day, just for the fun of it or out of boredom. In such case, those stances usually do not last—they come and go. On the other hand, when a horse is in discomfort or in pain he will usually move into a particular stance for a much longer period of time as it brings him relief.

Depending on the nature of the discomfort, the marked stance will appear sometimes shortly after an injury or sometimes days after. When muscles and fascia are irritated or traumatized, they contract, twist, and turn throughout the body, becoming rigid and losing their flexibility. Over several days, muscle compensation and fascia layers reorganize themselves along the lines of tension imposed on the body, providing support and protection from further pain. This is often referred to as compensation. Therefore, reading the stance of your horse can be revealing of new, or old, discomfort.

Most often a healthy horse stands on three legs, with one hind leg bearing little or no weight. It is part of their natural stance when resting, switching legs back and forth. If your horse persists on resting the same leg for hours it is a sign of some discomfort over that particular leg. Your horse might have strained a muscle or sprained a ligament, or is feeling the onset of some arthritic pain. Arthritis in a joint will cause some excessive heat in that joint, and eventual swelling. Use your palpation skills to identify the sorest spot on the entire leg, the compensatory muscular tension, and any associated fascial restrictions. Also check the size of the hoof in comparison to the other hoof; a smaller or even a contracted heel would definitely be a sign of something going on with that leg.

If your horse is standing with one hip higher, showing hypertonic muscles on the same side with his other hip dropped and the leg dangling underneath, you can suspect some serious musculoskeletal problem on that loose side. Use your palpation skills to identify the sorest spot on the leg, the compensatory muscular tension, and its associated fascial restrictions. Your horse might have a minor muscle strain or ligament sprain. It can also be a more serious problem such as a rupture of the peroneus tertius ligament or of the tibialis anterior muscle or even a fractured bone. In such case, your horse would display some trembling and sweating; immediately contact your veterinarian.

Figure 6.5 shows a horse standing *camped-under,* with his front legs farther back than normal and his hind legs farther forward under him than normal, it is most likely indicative of a backache, either of muscular or skeletal origin.

Use your palpation skills (see chapter 1) to determine the point of soreness and the associated compensatory muscular tension. Check the spinal vertebrae, the rib cage, and the belly. This stance can be developed following some muscle strain (overuse, ill-fitted saddle) or some bruising

*6.5 Horse Camped-Under*

(trauma, rolling over a stone). If the stance evolves to the point where your horse stands with his back slightly humped (*roached*), his abdominal muscles tight, and his head fixed in one position, it is a sure sign of body pain. This is known as splinting. The origin can range from serious muscle bruising, ribs out, or more serious problems such as pleurisy, peritonitis, or colic. If the horse paws the ground with his front feet or kicks his belly with his hind feet, it is a sure sign of colic. Contact your veterinarian immediately.

If after exercises, your horse is standing with his hind *camped out* in the back, as shown in figure 6.6, with his weight on the front legs, his head down and sweating, it could means that he is *tied up*.

Your palpation of the rump will reveal some muscle spasms and muscle tension all along the back, hence his stance. You need to keep your horse walking and warm, and to give him some electrolytes immediately. If you are not familiar with this condition, contact your veterinarian immediately.

If your horse is standing *camped out* but rigid, head up, eyes wide open, and ears back with an obvious facial expression of discomfort, you should suspect tetanus. Your palpation will probably reveal muscle spasms all over his body, and your horse will be hypersensitive to any touch or sound. Nowadays tetanus is a rare problem, thanks to vaccination. However, tetanus can be acquired from untended wounds. If you suspect it is the case, contact your veterinarian immediately.

When your horse is pointing, meaning he stands with one foreleg in front of the other, this stance is indicative of some forelimb discomfort.

*6.6 **Horse Camped Out, Tied Up***

Most often your horse takes this stance in order to relieve the weight from his flexor muscles, or his suspensory ligaments. This particular stance also allows the horse to open his shoulder joint, relieving his biceps muscle if strained, or relax a bruised point of shoulder. Sometimes the horse could also use this stance to relieve pressure from a sore elbow joint. Use your palpation skills to identify the sorest spot on the leg, the compensatory muscular tension, and its associated fascial restrictions.

When your horse is standing with his weight on one foreleg and the other foreleg bearing little or no weight at all, this is an indication that he experiences serious discomfort with the unweighted foreleg. It could be related to an underlying abscess, a puncture wound, possibly bad shoeing, or some arthritis. Use your palpation skills to identify the sorest spot on the leg, the compensatory muscular tension, and its associated fascial restrictions. If you cannot identify the source of the problem, check immediately with your veterinarian.

If your horse's stance is normal but he doesn't want to move his neck, this can be revealing of several problems ranging from muscle inflammation to misaligned vertebrae, possible arthritis, or an infection from an abscess in the skin or muscles. Use your palpation skills to identify the sorest spot on the neck, the compensatory muscular tension, and its associated fascial restrictions. If you do not understand the symptoms shown by your horse, consult your veterinarian. If your horse trembles and sweats, contact your veterinarian immediately.

When your horse switches his weight to the rear with his hind legs under and his rump and back muscles tense, he is avoiding pressure on his forelegs. This can be an indication of a very sore lower neck or withers, or a case of laminitis. Use your palpation skills to identify the sorest spot on the neck or withers, the compensatory muscular tension, and its associated fascial restrictions, if any. If your horse trembles and sweats, immediately contact your veterinarian.

Being able to recognize these stances will help you understand what your horse is showing you and where you will find his musculoskeletal and fascial stress, and assist you in identifying the myofascial restriction locations.

## WEIGHT DISTRIBUTION EVALUATION

How the horse distributes his weight between the fore and hind legs is of great importance. You can easily determine this by using the *float line*. Draw an imaginary line between the center of oscillation of the foreleg (upper third of scapula) and the center of articulation for the hind limb (point of hip), as illustrated in figure 6.7. This is called the float line and it should be close to horizontal.

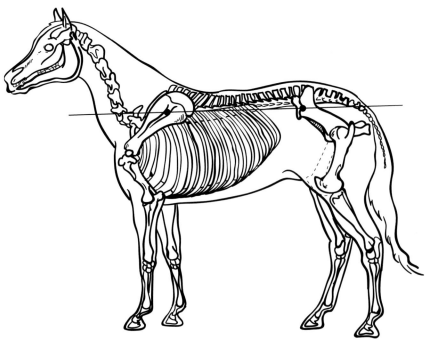

*6.7 Float Line Diagram*

The horse you are riding might have an "uphill balance" with his withers higher that his point of croup, or he might have a "downhill balance" with his point of croup higher than his withers. It is more desirable if the point of the foreleg were slightly higher than the point at the hind leg than if the reverse were true. When the point at the hind leg is slightly higher than the point of the foreleg, the weight of the horse tends to be distributed more toward the front end, causing it to be slightly out of balance and therefore apt to develop stress over his forelegs, leading to more serious problems such as inflammation of the muscle fibers, or worse, in the tendons, ligaments, and feet of the front quarters.

## SUMMARY

Knowledge of the various horse conformations and horse stances is a great advantage when evaluating your horse, especially a new horse. This very knowledge will help you develop a sharp eye to better read and understand a horse's conformation and stance while at rest. It will quickly become second nature and will enable you to locate more quickly the area of discomfort, if any. Review this chapter from time to time to help refresh your memory.

# THE RIDING EVALUATION
# PROGRAM (REP)

This section presents a Riding Evaluation Program, the REP, which will help riders of all levels determine the physical and mental fitness of any horse. For either the leisure or the sporting horse, the REP provides sufficiently varied work for you to evaluate the qualities inherent to that particular horse: suppleness, natural rhythm, impulsion, straightness, and collection. The REP will allow you to rediscover your horse's natural qualities, his weaknesses, and his peculiarities, and in the case of a prospective new horse, to evaluate his potential.

This easy riding evaluation program serves as a foundation for all riding levels. It will allow you to determine the natural performance limitations and identify any abnormalities present in your horse. The REP gives you a systematic and progressive program of gymnastics to successfully evaluate your horse physically and mentally at various gaits. This exercise sequence will help you separate behavioral from physical problems. The progression is logical, from easy to difficult. This will allow you to test his musculoskeletal system, and consider (or discover, in the case of a new prospect) the horse's individual natural talents and/or limitations. Do not hurry through the test. Let the horse move naturally and carry the movement.

The information contained in this second part of the book will help you recognize which side of the horse is the strongest and which side is the weakest, which muscle groups are tight and which joints, if any, are weak. This riding test is a matter of trial and error. As you proceed to work all natural gaits and their variations through the various exercises, you will be able to challenge all aspects of the horse's anatomy. As you gain experience with this process, you will make better assumptions about what you feel, see, and get from your horse's performance. However, they will still be guesses. You will be able to confirm these guesses with your palpation test, covered in the third part of this book.

The REP can also be used for helping a horse through a career transition (for example, when acquiring a horse from the track and then starting him in dressage or jumping training). Also, this exercise program can be used when rehabbing a horse from an injury. Regardless of the horse's level of training (or the rider's), use this exercise sequence to work the foundation of each gait. Take it apart, step by step, to evaluate each stride and see how your horse reacts to it. The REP helps you discover, or redis-cover, your animal and find solutions to actual problems.

## THE ARENA

The REP is designed to be practiced in a standard-size arena of 65 feet (20 meters) by 131 feet (40 meters). It's best if you're able to test your horse in a standard dressage arena of 65 feet (20 meters) by 196 feet (60 meters) because it gives you more space to practice these exercises. For the purpose of simplification, letters are positioned around the arena perimeter in the same fashion that is seen in the basic level of dressage. Each of the diagrams presented in this book is coded with these letters to help you better visualize and remember the patterns to be executed.

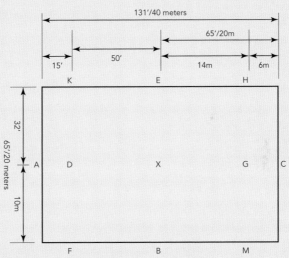

*Part II.1* **Standard Arena with Letters**

## THE NORMAL GAIT

For any of the gaits—walk, trot, or canter—always start riding your horse at his normal pace first. Do not interfere in any way, do not collect or lengthen the stride. The horse's normal gait will give you the best "read-ing" of his actual musculoskeletal fitness at that gait. Observing the purity of the three basic gaits is very important before moving to more elaborate movements and techniques. During the REP, the walk and canter gaits will give you the best evaluation of the skeletal system. If your horse shows problems during the walk and/or the canter, they will be hard to improve upon. The trot will help you more with the evaluation of the muscular and fascia system. Problems felt during the trot can be more easily improved upon with proper exercises.

## PRAISING

Throughout the REP, be generous with your praising of the horse. Every time the horse does what you want, tell him right away he did the right thing. Tell him you appreciate his effort, his good work, and his cooperation. Every chance you get, smile at him. Pet him with a soft touch. Make him feel special. This will "earn" you big points in developing a relationship with him, especially if it is a new horse you are riding.

## NEW HORSE

When trying a new horse, consider having him ridden by his owner or trainer before you proceed with the REP. This way you will have a chance to watch and note any abnormalities and/or qualities of that horse. First, ask for the horse to be ridden at all his normal gaits of walk, trot, and canter. The quality and the purity of the gait are most important. Then ask for all the variations and collected gaits. Also pay attention to the way the rider rides the horse. It will give you a good idea on what the horse is used to.

Is the rider soft with the horse or is he using strong aids?

Is he balanced or crooked?

Is he causing the horse to compensate? If yes, to what extent?

When you get on the horse, you might want to ride him in a similar fashion so the horse recognizes a similar very good routine, just with a different rider. However, after a few minutes, switch back to your style of riding. Develop a dialogue with the horse by asking him a few questions with your aids. How is your horse responding? To establish early contact, consider the walk–halt transitions (see page 105).

## THE HORSE'S DEMEANOR

Besides identifying the fitness level of your horse, the REP will also help you discover your horse's demeanor and work ethic.

Is your horse willing to work?

Is he showing good temperament?

Does he enjoy working?

Is he enthusiastic about working?

Is he devoted to his work?

Is he lazy, erratic, or temperamental?

Is he active and forward?

How does he behave when you mount him?

How is he leading out of the stables?

This thorough test will help you discover all those details so you can choose the right horse for you.

## RELAXING YOUR HORSE

When a horse is tense, his muscles are tight and his psyche is worried, confused, and/or afraid. A tense horse moves with general stiffness and feels uncomfortable. He might not relate to you to his best ability. But when a horse is relaxed, he is more confident; more willing to comply with your demands, and his body is suppler and more able to perform at its natural rhythm. Before starting the REP on any given horse, ensure the horse is relaxed. During your initial connection, especially with a new horse, consider applying the short version of the relaxation massage routine (see chapter 3) before riding. This great working opportunity gives you a chance to become attuned with the horse while relaxing him at the same time.

## PROPER TACK

Before starting the REP, make sure you use a saddle that properly fits your horse and that is comfortable to you. An ill-fitting saddle causes the horse soreness, resulting in his muscles tensing up and the development of muscle compensation. Thus the importance of a good and fitting saddle is crucial. Information on saddle fitting is beyond the scope of this book. If you need information on this topic, contact a qualified saddle-fitting expert. Also, check for the right bit. A good bit for your horse should be two-tenths of an inch wider than the mouth and set so the corner of the mouth shows a little wrinkle. To set the bit too high or too low will interfere with good contact. It is true that the stronger, more heavily built horse usually takes a firmer contact than the lighter, hot-blooded type. Always adjust the bit accordingly.

## SELF-SCRUTINY

Before you start testing your horse, ensure that you are properly positioned so you do not interfere with your horse's natural abilities. Sit straight and balanced in your saddle, putting even weight on your seat bones. Keep your leg aids light and be sure to release your squeezing action. Avoid tensing up, resulting in the clamping of your legs and arms, loosing the finesse of contact. Your aids, if not accurate, cause some of the abnormalities seen in the horse evaluation. Before drawing conclusions on any abnormality shown by your horse, verify your position and your aids. Consider riding several different exercises to verify the consistency of the problem.

# 7

## THE REP STARTING POINT

This chapter presents key points that both inexperienced and experienced riders should be aware of and comfortable with before starting the Riding Evaluation Program. Keep in mind also that it is important to differentiate the response to your aids from a young horse, such as a 3- or 4-year-old, from an older horse with more training. Have more patience with the younger, less experienced, and less obedient animal because his behavior might fluctuate during the REP. Such characteristics would not be acceptable from an older horse with more experience.

## CONTACT

In this context, contact refers to the connection between the horse's mouth and the rider's hands. As you establish contact with the horse's mouth, what is referred as to being "on the bit," keep your arms soft and flexible and, most important, even with both hands. Your contact should be elastic, not rigid or too loose. Avoid doing the seesaw motion that causes the bit to go back and forth in his mouth. Just take a minute to imagine how that would feel in your own mouth. Not a gentle way to establish communication. So keep your hands soft and ensure the horse loosens his neck, poll, and jaw before moving forward.

As you proceed in exercising the horse, always keep a balanced contact between your two reins, being gentle but present at the bit whenever you ask your horse to go forward, bend, turn, or stop. Use just enough pull to ride, not "front to back" but "back to front," bringing your horse alive, springing to your aids. Keep in mind that a firm contact through your reins is uncomfortable to your horse, and keeping it prolonged will most likely reduce his desire to go forward.

When a horse accepts the contact and complies willingly with your command, he engages his hindquarters and the rest of his body. On the other hand, if he feels pain, discomfort, or simply stiffness in any area of his anatomy, he might not accept your contact so easily. You might run into the following scenarios:

The horse is leaning on your hands, meaning he does not use his neck muscles sufficiently and lets you hold him instead. This is a sure sign of laziness and/or a noncompliant attitude.

The horse carries himself above the bit, with his neck and head raised. Usually you will feel a hollow back in this situation. Being above the bit can be indicative of discomfort in the mouth. If the horse tosses his head, it is a sure sign of discomfort or pain in the mouth (dentition), in the jaw (TMJ), or in the upper neck (possible misalignment of the first couple of cervical vertebrae), or all of the above.

The horse carries himself behind the bit. This may signify discomfort in the mouth (dentition) and/or in the jaw (TMJ). It can also reveal a fear of contact.

## BEING SQUARE

For a horse to be ideally square, he should stand motionless, on the bit, with his weight distributed evenly over all four legs. Also, his fore and hind legs should form a perfect rectangle underneath his forehand and his hindquarters.

*7.1 Standing Square*

From that stance, the horse should be ready to respond promptly to your aid's command. Before you engage in the REP, ask your horse to stand square. Then observe whether your horse is:

Standing evenly on all four legs?

Avoiding putting weight on one particular limb?

Forming a perfect rectangle between his fore and hind feet?

Comfortable with the bit?

Shaking his head?

Relaxed with his neck?

Showing the quality of calmness?

Restless, fussing, and/or pawing?

Performing this stance before your evaluation will already give you interesting feedback. Then consider repeating the "Being Square" stance when the horse is warm, near the end of your exercise session. Note if there is any difference and, if any, to what extent.

## STEPPING BACKWARD

Often termed *rein back*, this exercise asks the horse to move backward, as shown in figure 7.2.

This exercise often creates some anxiety in a horse, because it is not a natural movement for the horse. Horses usually do not like to move where they cannot see. So unless the horse is well trained, expect a little difficulty during the execution of this exercise. An interesting observation is that during that movement, the horse will move his legs in diagonal pairs, much like a trot, but at a walk. So, how does your horse respond to your "rein back" command?

Is the horse refusing to go in reverse? This unwillingness could be a sign of a problem in his spine, most likely his sacrum, or eventually his stifle or hocks. When the sacrum is at fault, usually the tail is clamped to the sore side.

When reining back, does your horse veer to one side? This may indicate discomfort on that side of the sacroiliac joint. It would contribute to slow work on that side.

Is the horse raising his neck and head, and slow-tensing his top line? This can be a sign of a dental problem, possibly TMJ, or simply some fearful character trait.

Is the horse rushing backward? If he does, and especially if he carries his head and neck down, this also could be a sign of dental, possibly TMJ or even cervical vertebrae problems.

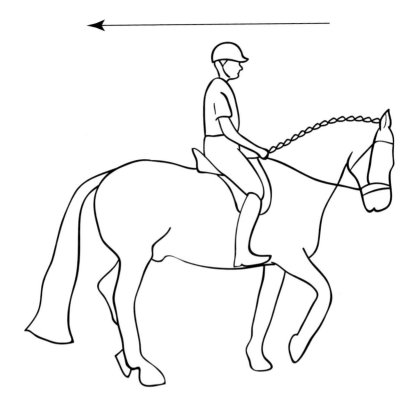

*7.2  Rein Back Exercise*

If your horse is capable of "reining back" without a problem, this is good news. If not, take note of the signs shown during this execution. Later, during your PEP, you will be able to manually check the key areas associated with his discomfort to verify their physical condition.

## IMPULSION

A horse's impulsion is his forward response to your leg aids. A good impulsion arises when a horse really swings from his hindquarters. So as you gently squeeze your legs around your horse's ribcage to activate your horse's hindquarters, you can evaluate his impulsion:

Does your horse have good impulsion?

If his impulsion is strong, does it make you feel he is taking you places? If yes, it usually is a sign of good and sound structure.

Is his impulsion mild, lacking "oomph"? If yes, it could mean that he has weak hind muscles or some discomfort in his skeletal structure.

To develop impulsion, consider working on a lot of short tempo changes. Ride forward a few yards, then collect for a few more and relax;

repeat several times. You should not find yourself having to kick again and insist to get the forward motion. This exercise should reveal to you quickly if your horse is:

Not responsive to your leg aids, being lazy or placid: If you have to insist to get some impulsion, this indicates a horse lacking impulsion.

Mildly responsive to your leg aid, or being dull: This dullness can be positively influenced to change with regular exercise and training.

Proper response, an impulsion that makes you feel he is taking you places.

Ultraresponsive to your leg aids, being alert: This indicates a strong condition, being hot, almost impatient. With regular exercise and training, this condition can be positively influenced to change.

Impulsion is a direct reflection of your horse's engine (hindquarters). The energy generated by his engine can be harnessed and channeled in different ways. However, a horse with no impulsion will be a tough act to see through.

## RHYTHM

As your horse moves through the various gaits, pay close attention to the rhythm he shows. This may help you detect the little flaws that lead to identifying the real problem.

Develop a feel for the rhythmic cadence of the four-beat walk gait, the two-beat trot gait, and the three-beat canter gait. Is each step sounding even? Listen well. When you detect an uneven rhythm from the fore or the hinds, this can be due to:

His innate "sidedness," with either right or left side being dominant and the opposite side being weaker: This can be addressed and adjusted with a good training program.

Some form of lameness affecting one leg more than the other: This can be traced to joints not bending properly due to arthritis or inflammation. In such case, you need your veterinarian to evaluate the limb and provide the best course of treatment.

Rhythm mistakes are often connected with problems such as contact at the mouth, the tension of the reins, and/or a tight back. A horse can only move in a pure rhythm if his back swings smoothly and his neck and back muscles contract and relax without force. A relaxed horse bends and extends his joints equally, and he appears content.

Keep in mind that good conformation, meaning balanced proportions, will influence the ability of the horse to be naturally rhythmical. An underdeveloped musculature in a horse, regardless of age, can cause him difficulty in maintaining good rhythm. Proper training can adjust that.

## IS YOUR HORSE "JIGGING" AT WALK?

When a horse moves or bobs up and down jerkily and rapidly, it is known as *jigging* and is considered a false trot. Jigging is a sign of rashness, of excess energy, and/or of tension. Jigging can be of physical origin if there is some musculoskeletal restriction. Jigging can also be due simply to the horse's attitude or lack of education. Usually, regular exercise, as well as turn out, will contribute to relax this type of horse.

# INSIDE–OUTSIDE

The terms inside and outside simply refer to the horse's body position in relationship to the line of travel. For example, when turning to the right, clockwise, the inside is the right side of the horse and the outside is the left side of the horse, as shown in figure 7.3.

When you travel to the left, counterclockwise, the horse's left side is considered the inside and his right side is considered the outside. Is your horse's natural balance going to the left or to the right? Usually a horse will naturally "pull" toward the tighter, or weaker, side of his body.

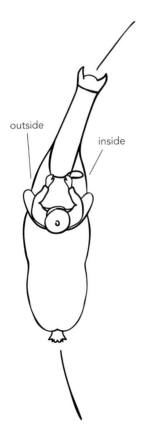

*7.3 Inside-Outside Diagram*

outside

inside

# STRAIGHTNESS

By definition, straightness refers to the straight alignment of the horse's entire spine. In other words, the poll, the withers, the spine, the sacrum, and the tail are all aligned. However, "textbook" straightness is rare. Your horse is straight when he moves straight on a straight track and bends on curved lines as those may require, not bulging out to the outside or falling in the inside, wandering off the center line. His hind feet move in the track of the front feet (see chapter 9, page 90). Straightness comes from the balance the horse develops in his hindquarters.

Horses, like humans, have a dominant side. Which side is dominant in your horse?

Why is it important to know a horse's dominant side? Be aware that the muscles on the nondominant side will be slightly weaker than the muscles on the dominant side. This will often result in the dominant side showing less range of motion during action due to the tighter muscle tone. The nondominant side being weaker will result in awkward movements, often resembling "crookedness."

*Important fact:* Often when traveling a straight line, a horse will naturally shift his haunches slightly to the inside of the line of travel. This is due to his anatomical structure; since his hindquarters are larger than his shoulders, his hind legs are set wider than his shoulders. This anatomical feature gives the horse a wedge–shaped form, causing him to compensate by shifting his haunches. This can be easily corrected by bringing the horse's shoulder in line with his haunches.

So, as you walk, ask yourself the following questions:

Is my horse straight?

Does his tail remain straight?

Are his haunches drifting inside?

Does he bend to one side in particular?

If your horse moves somewhat crookedly, it may simply mean that he is not balanced in his hindquarters. One of his sides is working harder, usually creating a "rounded" side. The "hollow" side is the one the horse favors by using it less. Shoulder-in exercises are recommended to correct this natural crookedness. When riding, concentrate on the hind legs. The more equally both hind legs follow the path of the front legs, the stronger and more balanced the hindquarters become.

## STRAIGHTNESS IN TURNS

During a turn, the horse should conform to the curved line that his feet are traveling on. When this happens, you can say the horse is in optimal balance. If not, which side is at fault? Is it the inside or the outside?

## COLLECTION

When collecting your horse, you ask him to carry more weight on his hindquarters, by lifting his hind legs equally in direction of his center of gravity located in midthorax, at the level of the eighth rib. This increases the joint action and power generated by the hinds. During collection, the horse lowers his croup somewhat and raises his poll. If the horse has difficulty collecting himself in a frame, this can indicate a skeletal problem either from the spine or from the hind limbs, or both, In such instances, contact your veterinarian chiropractor for a thorough evaluation of your horse's skeletal system and to provide appropriate treatment.

## STRETCHING THE NECK DURING THE REP

Stretching the neck should be allowed frequently at any stage of the REP. It is a good way to keep your horse relaxed and happy. It also helps you maintain maximum contact. To stretch your horse's neck, allow him to walk with his neck long and low, without falling on the forehand. Keep constant contact with the horse's mouth. As the expression says, let him "chew the reins out of your hands." It is beneficial to do this type of neck stretch frequently for short periods of time because it allows the horse to round and stretch his back.

Understanding the key points presented above will help you differentiate the minor problem from the more serious one during your Riding Evaluation Program. In the long run, it will save you time and money.

# 8

## SIGNS OF PROBLEMS WITH YOUR HORSE

This chapter describes signs associated with some of the most common conditions seen in the horse. This information will help you better detect and understand your horse's condition. Absorbing this information will help you quickly recognize these common problems during the application of both the REP and the PEP. Make sure to come back to this chapter from time to time to refresh your memory.

## BACK PROBLEMS

Back problems can range from mild inflammation of the muscles and associated fascia, to more severe conditions such as spinal misalignment, kissing spines, head of ribs sticking out, and arthritis in the vertebrae. The palpation evaluation program presented in the third part of this book shows you how to identify these various structures. If you suspect some skeletal misalignment, contact your veterinarian chiropractor to relieve the problem immediately.

The most common back problem is condition known as *cold back*. A cold back describes an inflammation of the back muscles, associated fasciae, and sometimes the spinal ligament. A horse that noticeably flinches when being massaged, groomed, or saddled could be subject to an early case of cold back.

If your horse hollows his back in an attempt to avoid the discomfort, this is a sure sign of an achy back. Other symptoms such as crankiness and being "girthy" when saddled and/or mounted are also sure signs of back problems. Another giveaway is when a rider seats abruptly and heavily in the saddle and the horse reacts violently. When being ridden, a horse with a back problem will be reluctant to:

Go forward
Bend in one or both directions
Extend his back

Lengthen his stride

Transition from trot to canter

Change canter leads

Riding without a properly fitted saddle is most often responsible for back problems. Occasionally, bad riding can be also a source of soreness for the back structures. The combination of the two is most often the real origin of this common problem.

Another important factor in back problems is weak abdominal muscles. The interplay of the back and abdominal muscles is what allows the horse to have a strong bridge between the hindquarters and the forehand. If one of the two muscle groups is weak, it will automatically affect the other. By strengthening the abdominal muscles you will contribute to relieving the back muscle tightness.

## DIFFICULTY IN ENGAGING THE HINDQUARTERS

When your horse has difficulty in engaging his hindquarters, you can trace the origin to:

A lumbosacral misalignment

Joint problems; DJD (degenerative joint disease)

Improper shoeing, long toe/low heel, and associated fasciae

Tight gluteal and hamstring muscles

If your horse presents difficulty in engaging his hinds during the REP, please be thorough over his back and hindquarters during your PEP.

## HEAD TOSSING

When a horse tosses his head in the air regularly, he often does that in an attempt to stretch part of his neck, or its entirety. Head tossing is often associated with:

Upper cervical misalignment between the first cervical vertebra and the occipital portion of the skull; sometimes between the first and the second cervical vertebrae

Some dental problems

The wrong bit

ETDS (Equine Temporomandibular Dysfunction Syndrome)

The legs swinging outward (paddling) or inward (winging) during gait pattern

If the horse only tosses his head when you ask for a transition, this most likely reveals a mouth problem of either the bit or some dental issues, including ETDS.

## Neck Problems

A good neck is one of the horse's most important features. When a horse moves, he uses his neck and head to keep the rest of his body in balance for optimal performance. He raises his neck when extending his spine or during "collection work"; he moves his neck laterally during turns, circles, and lateral work; he flexes his neck during extension or to stretch his back. Also, the neck must be flexible at the poll. A long neck gives a horse a mechanical advantage in balancing himself by making a wide range of adjustments along the length of his body during movement. It works very well especially if the horse is well developed in his hindquarters. However, a long neck is often stiff and tight because of the weight of the head. A short neck is often tight with more difficulty to lateral bending and flexing at the poll.

Here are some signs of neck problems:

If your horse has difficulty moving his neck properly, it can be simply due to muscle tightness on one or both sides of the neck.

If your horse can move his neck to one side but refuses to move to the other, it can be due to a misalignment (subluxation) in his lower cervical vertebrae.

If your horse tosses his head in the air regularly and consistently to the same side, it is usually due to an upper cervical vertebrae misalignment (see "Head Tossing," page 87).

## Refusal to Pick up a Canter

When a horse refuses to engage into a canter, regardless of the lead, it is a serious sign of a physical problem in the joints of the limbs, problems such as arthritis, or other inflammatory problems in the lower leg.

## Taking the Bit

When a horse takes the bit and disregards your commands, this can indicate:

Cervical misalignment

C7–T1 misalignment and first rib syndrome

Possibly other vertebrae due to the strong push from behind

Dental problem

Possible ETDS (Equine Temporomandibular Joint Dysfunction Syndrome)

Being able to recognize the signs associated with these most common conditions will help you to evaluate your horse's physical condition more quickly during your riding evaluation program.

# 9

## THE RIDING EVALUATION
## PROGRAM (REP) EXERCISES

The REP presents a series of exercises that will help you to progressively test all aspects of your horse's musculoskeletal makeup. These exercises are considered the foundation of riding. Some exercises are done at walk, some at trot and/or canter, and some at all gaits. Riding your horse through these simple exercises will tell you a lot about your horse's fitness and his demeanor. The horse responds differently with each exercise, depending on the difficulty of execution.

Follow the REP's recommended sequences to assess your horse's strength and weakness of movement. This purposely structured riding test will give you opportunities to challenge your horse's entire musculoskeletal system in a safe and enjoyable way. As your horse moves through the exercises, you will be able to judge his aptitude and weakness as well as his character.

Most exercises presented here, like any gymnastic exercises, are fatiguing to the horse. Keep in mind when testing your horse that fatigue and tension will disrupt his rhythm, especially at walk and trot. So for each exercise, keep the number of strides minimal so you can see the horse moving at his normal and best rhythm. Become attuned to his body language. Change direction frequently and do not hesitate to give him a walking break.

Before drawing conclusions on any abnormality shown by your horse during a particular exercise, consider riding several different exercises to verify the consistency of the possible issue at hand.

The REP will help you determine at what level of fitness your horse is. With a new horse, this process will allow you to see what his character is like: quiet or excitable, generous or not, hearted or distant. But, most importantly, it is an opportunity to evaluate his overall musculoskeletal fitness and his potential. The REP will help you identify if that particular new horse is what you are looking for. When looking at a new horse, you should assume he will not change. If you detect some major flaws, don't expect them to be fixed. It is like a pair of uncomfortable shoes at the store—they don't get any better. However, if the horse moves well, his muscular fitness can always be improved. It is what makes horse riding so interesting.

## EXERCISE 1: STRAIGHT LINES

This first exercise gives you an outline of straight lines to carry out first at a horse's normal walk, trot, and canter. This exercise will allow you to warm up the horse while evaluating the symmetry of his gaits, his forwardness, and his straightness. Later in the progression of the REP you will be able to try the different variations at each gait.

Entering the arena at A, walk the horse straight to C, then turn left and follow the rail all the way around the arena, passing corner 2, points H, E, K, and corner 1. Then at point A, bend your horse left again and walk straight to C. Then bend your horse to the right and head toward corner 3, pass points M, B, F, and corner 4, then back to point A, where you are ready for the next exercise.

## EXERCISE 2: HALF CIRCLES AND FIGURE-8S

Riding your horse in a half circle is a good exercise to verify his flexibility. When a horse bends, the muscles on the inside of the circle contract, and the muscles on the outside stretch. The play between the muscle groups is what allows the horse to conform smoothly to the arc

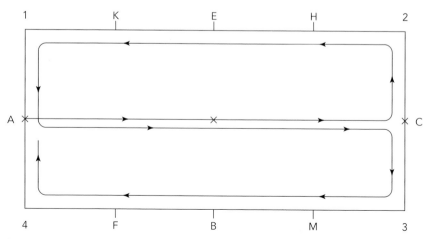

*9.1 Exercise 1: Straight Lines Diagram*

of the circle you chose to ride. Keep in mind that the spine of a horse has little to no lateral bending capability. So when a horse refuses to bend to one side, it could indicate a spinal issue, such as a subluxation, that can trigger discomfort ranging from mild to severe. Riding half circles will help you discover the horse's natural crookedness, his preferred side, which is more flexible; the other side will be stiffer.

The horse's sense of balance is really challenged during curves. Therefore it is important to proceed to some self-scrutiny before you start assessing your horse on half circles. Make sure you are sitting evenly on your seat bones, well in the middle of your saddle. Keep your rein contact even and soft, with your inside rein lightly flexing the horse poll in direction of the bend and your outside rein guarding his outside neck and shoulder. Keep your legs gently wrapped around his rib cage with your inside leg acting as a post around which the horse turns, and your outside leg slightly behind the girth to ensure the hindquarters do not move to the outside.

As you follow the outline shown in figure 9.2, you will be executing half circles on a radius of 30 feet (10 meters). This will gently bend your horse and affect his musculature strongly, both in stretching the muscles on the outside of his body during the circle, and in exercising strong contractions of the muscles on the inner aspect of his body as he turns in the circle. The figure-8 exercise is simply the execution of the two circles incorporating changes of direction at the midpoint.

Starting at point A, walk toward point K in a nice half circle that will end in the middle of the arena X. Once there, change reins and duplicate the half circle going toward M and ending on C. Keep going on the same rein and repeat the same exercise in the same fashion, making your way toward H, through the center of the arena X with a change of reins, to F, and finish at A, ready for the next exercise.

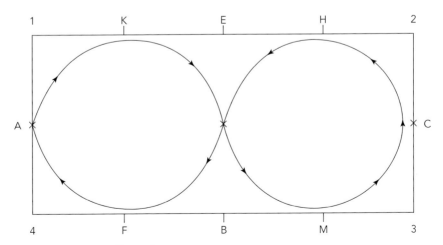

*9.2 Exercise 2: Half Circles*

A variation to this half-circle exercise is to ride at the posting trot using both the correct and the incorrect diagonals to feel the "difference" and see if the horse is lame or uncomfortable on any direction or diagonal at the rider's rising trot (see chapter 10, page 107).

## EXERCISE 3: SERPENTINES

The serpentine exercise is an excellent exercise to develop suppleness and balance, and therefore is a great opportunity to further test your horse's flexibility. "Serpentine" is the name given to a series of half circles put together in an S shape, as seen in figure 9.4. During the serpentine exercise you will be doing half circles that are half the radius of the

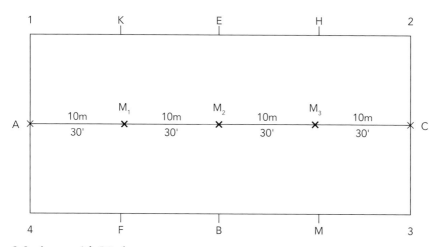

*9.3 Arena with Markers*

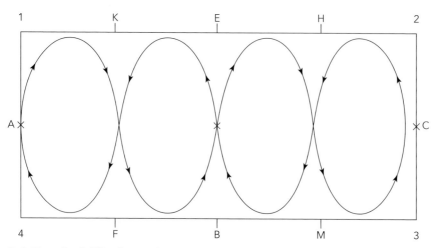

*9.4 Exercise 3: The Serpentine Diagram*

last exercise. This exercise will really get your horse moving with a lot of lateral flexion, increasing the degree of bending, affecting the deeper muscle and fascia layers, which will be alternately worked and stretched. It will help you further determine if your horse is even on both sides, which side is stronger and/or more flexible. For the same reasons expressed in exercise 2, proceed to some self-scrutiny to ensure the correct use of your seat and aids before proceeding with the serpentine exercise.

Until you are accustomed to the distance in this exercise I suggest you have a marker every 30 feet (10 meters), for a total of three markers along the median line of the arena. This will help you appreciate the distances at which you need to cross the median line, as shown in figure 9.3.

Starting at point A, move toward point K and, observing a radius of good 15 feet (5 meters), bend your horse to the right toward the first marker (M1) on the ground. As you pass the first marker, change rein and bend to the left in another radius of 15 feet (5 meters) toward the second marker (M2). As you pass the second marker, change rein and bend your horse to the right another radius of 15 feet (5 meters) toward the third marker (M3). As you pass the third marker, change rein and bend your horse to the left in another radius of 15 feet (5 meters) toward point C. You have completed a serpentine of four short radius bends, two to the right and two to the left. Keep going on the same rein and duplicate the exercise in the same fashion, making your way back and crossing the median lane three times and finish on A, ready for the next exercise.

## EXERCISE 4: LATERAL WORK WITH LEG YIELD

Lateral work is a great way to test the balance and suppleness of your horse. In training, the leg yield exercise is used to strengthen the horse's inside hind leg, to develop straightness, and to increase the carrying power needed in the hindquarters for collected work. The hind leg has to bend more and bear more weight. It also causes more of a bend in the horse's midsection, working his muscle on the inside and stretching the one on the outside, strengthening the hollow side and loosening the stiff side.

Here in the REP, we use it to evaluate the horse's midsection and hind legs. This exercise will help you identify the horse's stronger and weaker sides. The leg yield movement causes the horse to move forward and sideways. During the leg yield exercise, performed at a walk and a trot, the horse steps forward and sideways, moving away from your inside leg, causing him to lightly flex away from the direction of movement. This puts greater pressure on all the joints of that hind leg. Any discomfort in hock and/or stifle would result in poor lateral movement. It is a good exercise to evaluate the suppleness of the horse's musculature and see if he is equally strong in both directions.

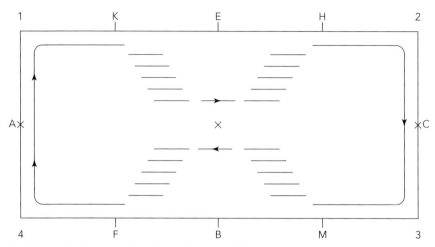

*9.5  Exercise 4: Lateral Work with Leg Yield Diagram*

Start at point A and bend right through corner 1. When you arrive at point K, apply your left leg as "front leg" to cause the horse to change diagonal for yield and flexion, almost as if you would use the "wrong" diagonal. Apply the front leg for a total of five steps, which will bring you to approximately 24 feet (9 meters) from the rail. Then move straight, parallel to the rail.

As you pass point E, apply your right leg as the "front leg" to change diagonal for yield and flexion, again in the "wrong" diagonal for five steps until you reach point H. Then keep straight along the rail, bend through corner 2, pass point C, and bend through corner 3; when you reach point M, repeat the same exercise. Use your left leg to initiate five inward steps. Go straight while moving parallel to the rail. Then use your right leg to initiate five outward steps going to point F. Then keep straight along the rail, bend through corner 4, pass point A, and as you approach corner 1 bend your horse to the right and take a change of diagonal across the arena to corner 3. During the diagonal, lengthen your reins some while maintaining contact, yet allowing your horse to relax his neck. As you reach corner 3, bend your horse around your leg to the left and repeat the entire loop of exercise 4 on the other rein.

Pass point C, through corner 2, bend with right leg yielding for five steps from point H straight pass point E, then left leg yield five steps to point K, through corner 1, pass point A into corner 4, bend with right leg yield five steps from point F, straight pass point B, then left leg yield five steps to point M. Then pass corner 3, point C, and just before corner 2, bend your horse to the left and take a diagonal across the arena to corner 4, where you will reposition yourself at point A, ready to begin the next exercise.

# EXERCISE 5: LATERAL WORK WITH SHOULDER-IN

This lateral work with the shoulder-in is another good exercise for testing the balance and suppleness of your horse. During the shoulder-in exercise, the horse's shoulders are brought to the inside of the hindquarter's line of travel. This exercise strengthens the inside hind leg muscles as well as the muscles of inside midsection. At the same time, it elongates the muscles on the outside of the midsection. If you perceive some issues during the shoulder-in exercise, it could be revealing some weakness in the hinds and/or midsections and back musculature, or even the skeleton.

Starting at point A, go in the direction of the corner 1, bend your horse to the right, past point K, past the center of the arena (X), past point F, and back to point A, completing your first circle to the right. Keep going toward point K. Then as you pass K, ride your horse forward, shoulder-in to the right on a straight-line past point E, and all the way to point H. Observe how your horse is carrying himself in this shoulder-in. Then bend to the right and pass corner 2. When you reach point C, bend to the right again and move straight to point A with loose rein to give your horse time to relax his back and neck. Then as you reach point A, bend your horse to the left toward corner 4 and point F past the center of the arena (X), past point K, back to point A, completing your first circle to the left. Continue until you pass point F, then ride your horse forward, shoulder-in to the right on a straight line, past point B all the way to point M. Observe how your horse is carrying himself in this shoulder-in. Then bend to the left and pass corner 3. When you reach point C, bend to the left again and move straight to point A with loose rein to give your horse time to relax his back and neck.

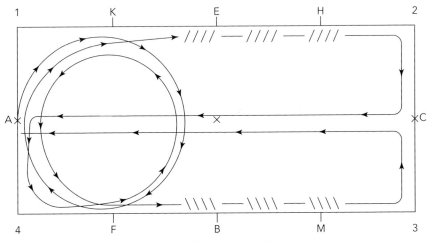

*9.6 Exercise 5: Lateral Work with Shoulder-in Diagram*

# 10

## THE WALK

In human relations, it is often said that the first impression is a lasting impression. When testing a horse, especially for the first time, the walk is your first impression of his abilities. During the warm-up phase, the walk will give you a lot of interesting feedback.

The walk is the best gait to use when checking for weak or sore muscles, because the muscles are relaxed and move freely during this action. A swinging horse at a walk is a good sign. If your horse does not "swing" underneath your seat, if he is tense with a choppy walk, and especially if he flips his head up, it is a sign of muscle tightness, possibly skeletal soreness, or tension.

Be aware that if there is some restriction of muscular origin, you will see it readily at the walk, whereas during the trot the overall action of the muscles (working as a unit) would mask any specific muscle tension (i.e., the horse "works out" of the soreness).

In a typical walk, the legs move in lateral pairs on the same side. For example, if you start the walk with the right front, the horse follows with the left hind, then the front left, followed by the right hind and back to the right front, completing the stride. Start walking your horse for a few minutes using exercise 1 (for details, see chapter 9, page 90), following the path shown in figure 10.1.

## THE NATURAL WALK

Walk your horse with loose reins, allowing the horse to stretch his neck long and low, let him walk until he finds his natural rhythm, the pace at which he moves most easily and naturally.

Be sure to maintain a constant contact with the horse's mouth, because you do not want to let him fall on the forehand (see chapter 7, pages 78–79). Let him "chew the reins out of your hands," as it is said. This will allow him to round his back. Be observant of his impulsion.

96

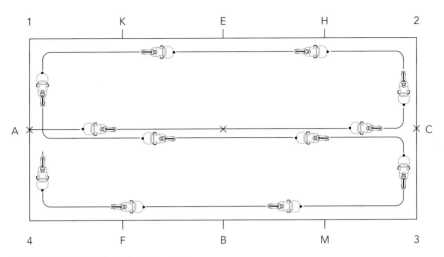

*10.1  Walk the Straight Line Diagram*

When asking your horse to walk, is he:

Moving forward with an attitude of perkiness?
Being energetic and loose?
Moving forward, but in a sluggish manner?
Focused on the task at hand?
"Dreamy" about his surroundings?

*10.2  The Natural Walk*

Pay attention to these details at this trial contact. It is indicative of the horse's character and demeanor. A horse must feel comfortable walking. His regularity of movement should be even, with his head nodding rhythmically to each lateral step. Is this the case with your horse?

This natural action should be evident. If the horse does not nod, if he keeps his neck stiff, it could be revealing of some cervical discomfort. If the horse tosses his neck occasionally or regularly, it is a sure sign of neck or jaw (TMJ) discomfort. In the second part of this book, you will discover how you can evaluate your horse's neck and jaw by using your hands. In the meantime, as you walk, check and see:

Is your horse moving easily and freely?

Is his rhythm slow or short and quick?

Is he balanced equally in front and behind?

Is he moving evenly in the shoulders and hips?

As your horse moves your hips and lower back, is that movement balanced and in rhythm?

Do you feel a dominant side? Which one?

Can you feel the horse's back swing underneath your seat?

Is the horse's back solid or is it hollow?

Is he flipping his head up? (Could be related to teeth, cervical vertebrae, or sacrum problems?)

Does he carry his head low?

Being able to read your horse's walk will reveal a lot about his musculoskeletal condition. A horse that is a little sore will be slightly "off," moving his legs unevenly. As the horse lifts each leg separately during the course of a stride (a complete cycle of limb movements), you should be able to feel how strong he is with each limb. Any discrepancies should be noted. Does any leg feel "off"? Is he dragging a leg?

Any shifting in the movement can indicate a chronic compensatory phenomenon that masks a deeper problem. Are the feet lifted clear off the ground or is he dragging them?

In a typical walk, the legs move in lateral pairs on the same side. For example, if you start the walk with the right front, the horse follows with the left hind, then the front left, followed by the right hind and back to the right front completing the stride.

Check the length of stride and the rhythmic cadence of the four-beat gait at the walk.

Is his four-beat rhythm balanced? Are the steps rhythmically even (one, two, three, four), or is there an irregularity (such as one, two-three, four)? If the rate of repetition of his steps—his tempo—is irregular, it could mean that he is avoiding pain at one particular point. Identifying the limb involved with the irregular tempo will help narrow down the area of potential problem.

If it is possible to walk the horse on a hard surface, the sound made by the hooves hitting the ground should be clear and rhythmic. Any differences in sound can reveal potential issues, from a shoeing problem to leg conformation.

*Lateral walk:* As you push your horse to walk faster, the rhythmic four-beat walk will become a "lateral walk," where the legs move in lateral pairs instead of separately. This is the rhythm seen with the "pacers" at the track. Repeat the exercise shown in figure 10.1. Is your horse comfortable with this lateral walk? Standardbred horses love this walk. However, other breeds might not enjoy it so readily. Some disciplines, such as dressage, do not like the horses using the lateral walk.

## READING YOUR TRACKS

It is to your advantage to walk your horse over a freshly groomed footing so you can read his tracks. Ride your horse at his normal walk and circle back so you can look at the pattern of hoofprints. When looking at these tracks the first belong to the hinds and the second to the fore. Front feet leave wider prints than the hinds.

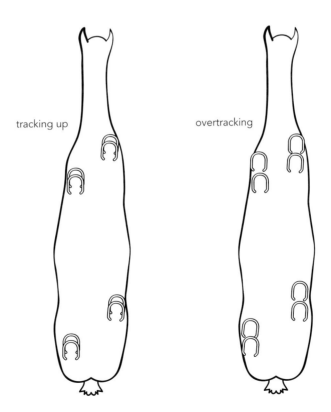

*10.3  The Horse Tracks: Tracking Up and Overtracking*

A balanced horse should be "tracking up," meaning his hind hoof prints should be stepping into the prints of his forefeet or beyond. This indicates that your horse's strides are sufficiently forward and free moving.

If your horse fails to track up, meaning his hinds do not reach the foreleg hoof prints, this is a sign of stiffness in his hinds, and possibly in his back and hips.

If your horse is overtracking, it is a good sign that the horse is supple, with free and ample movement in his hindquarters and back. Overtracking is often seen in tall horses with big strides, such as warm bloods and tall thoroughbreds.

If you do not have access to freshly groomed footing, consider walking in large 60-foot (20-meter) circles so you can look over your inside shoulder and supervise your tracks as you go.

## CURVE

As you know it is more difficult for a horse to maintain his balance on turns and curved lines. This might cause him to speed up or to slow down, and sometimes both depending on the situation at hand. To find out how your horse behaves in curves, challenge him to walk some large curves described in exercise 2 (see chapter 9, page 90). Follow the route shown in figure 10.4.

As you follow that pattern, you will be executing circles on a radius of 30 feet (10 meters). This will gently bend your horse and affect his musculature strongly, both in stretching the muscles on the outside of his body during the circle and in exercising strong contractions of the muscles on the inner aspect of his body as he turns in the circle. Here are some questions to ask yourself as you're riding:

Is your horse speeding up, slowing down, or both?

To which curve is the horse reacting the most, the left or the right?

When you bend to the left, is his curve a smooth bend throughout his entire spine, conforming to the arc of the circle, or is it not? Does it break at the poll, the lower neck, in midback, or by the hip?

When you bend to the right, is his curve a smooth bend throughout his entire spine, conforming to the arc of the circle, or is it not? Does it break at the poll, the lower neck, in midback, or by the hip?

How is your horse conforming to the arc of your circle?

Is your horse falling in or bulging out of the circle? This can indicate a balance issue due to skeletal problems.

Does the horse have a difficulty in a particular direction? If yes, which one?

Is his tempo affected in one direction more than the other?

Is he showing the same problem on both directions?

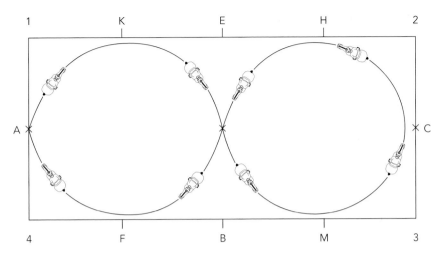

*10.4  Walk the Loose Curves Diagram*

Is his neck and forehand bending smoothly? If not, it could indicate a cervical vertebra problem.

Are the hindquarters conforming to the bend? If not, it could indicate a lumbar or sacral vertebra problem, even both.

Is his body falling in or out of the circle?

You can consider increasing the difficulty of this exercise by moving on to exercise 3 (see chapter 9, page 92). Follow the outline showed in figure 10.5. This exercise will really get your horse moving with a lot of lateral flexion as you will be doing half circles that are half the radius of the last exercise. The result is an increased degree of bending, affecting the deeper muscle and fascia layers, which will be alternately worked and stretched.

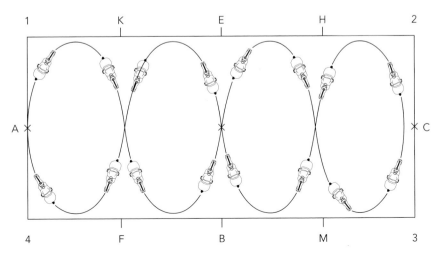

*10.5  Walk the Serpentine Diagram*

Is your horse even? If not, which side is stronger? Is your horse's straightness affected? Are your horse's hindquarters traveling outside or inside of the line of travel?

Be aware of the horse's hind legs. They should be properly lifted, then coming forward underneath the horse's belly, and the hooves should hit the ground flat. If it is the case, you know the hind legs are sound from the hip down to the fetlock. If one of the toes is not rolling over properly, it can be a shoeing problem. If the toe is dragging it could be a sign of some articulation deficiency (stifle or hock).

If you observe any of these instances, make a note of it, and later you will be able to verify during the trot. It is a good way to find out about old suspensory ligament injuries, if any. If you feel the problem is showing on the inside leg, it will confirm that the horse has some articulation problems. If it happens with the outside leg, the same problem is worse.

## WALK VARIATIONS

After you have evaluated your horse walking, try these variations in order to evaluate his ability to compress or to lengthen his stride and the outline of his body.

### THE MEDIUM WALK

The medium walk is the natural progression from the normal walk. Confirm your rein contact by bringing your horse on the bit and slightly increase his stride, making sure your horse is properly overtracking. Maintain the regular four-beat rhythm in an easy and unhindered manner.

*10.6 The Medium Walk*

*10.7* ***The Collected Walk***

## THE COLLECTED WALK

When you ask your horse to collect himself, you are asking him to redistribute his weight so he carries more over his hindquarters and less over his forehand, resulting in a walk that is more upward and not just outward. Your horse looks more active, yet has shorter strides than the extended walk. Repeat figures 10.1 and 10.3. Proper collection means that the horse has total balance over all four legs.

How does your horse collect himself?

Are his hind legs easily getting closer together and coming further under his center of gravity as he travels?

Does your horse have "carrying power"?

Is he bouncing off the ground? Or is he not so bouncy?

Do you feel his cadence, meaning his suspension capability in time?

If the horse has a hard time maintaining a collection, this indicates a deeper problem than just muscles. It could be a joint issue such as DJD (degenerative joint disease) or a misalignment (subluxation) in his spine. How does your horse hold his balance?

## THE EXTENDED WALK

The extended walk will allow you to test your horse's maximum length of stride, while keeping his head and neck stretched. You should see a noticeable overtracking with his hind feet.

*10.8* ***The Extended Walk***

See how your horse responds to your commands. Are his steps still even? Is his tracking changing? If the horse has problems lengthening his walk and stretching out his neck and head, it indicates muscular and/or facial stiffness, and eventually some joint stiffness (arthritis). Repeat the figure 10.1. If your horse does not have any problem lengthening his walk, it is a good sign.

## THE WALK LEG YIELD EXERCISE

Performed at a walk, the leg yield is a good exercise to evaluate the suppleness of the horse musculature. Ask your horse to step forward and sideways, moving away from your inside leg, causing him to lightly flex away from the direction of movement. See if he is equally strong in both directions.

Engage in exercise 4 (see chapter 9, page 93) and follow the outline shown in figure 10.9 to verify the following:

Is your horse as supple to the left leg yield as he is to the right?

Are his steps measured and even?

Do you see his inside eye, or is his neck not bending enough? This could reveal deep muscular tension on both sides of the neck.

Is the horse crooked with his haunches moving sideways? This could reveal some lumbar or sacral discomfort. Be sure it is not caused by your inside leg being too far back.

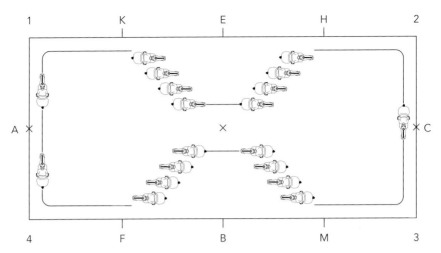

*10.9 The Walk Leg Yield Exercise Diagram*

## THE SHOULDER-IN EXERCISE

Performed at a walk, where the horse's shoulders are brought to the inside of the hindquarter's line of travel, the shoulder-in exercise will help you to test the inside hind leg muscles as well as the muscles of the inside midsection. At the same time, it elongates the muscles on the outside of the midsection. If you perceive some issues during the shoulder-in exercise, it could indicate some weakness in the hinds and/or midsection musculature, or even the skeleton. Engage in exercise 5 (see chapter 9, page 95) and follow the outline shown in figure 10.10 to verify the following:

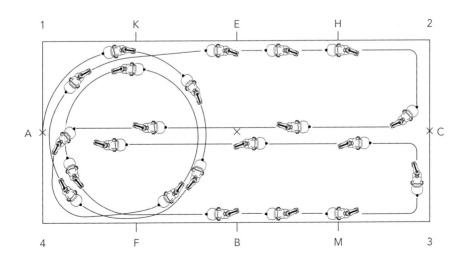

*10.10 The Walk Shoulder-in Exercise Diagram*

Is your horse as supple to the left shoulder-in as he is to the right shoulder-in?

Are his steps even?

Is his neck curved properly or is he uncomfortable?

Is your horse bending nicely? If not, it could indicate some lumbar or sacral discomfort. Be sure it is not caused by your inside leg being too far back.

# TRANSITIONS

During transitions, up or down, the horse switches gaits. In order to maintain his balance during the "switch," the horse has to contract all his muscle groups and ligaments. This makes transition very interesting when evaluating your horse. Difficulty during certain transitions will help you identify the area of concern for your horse. It is well known that to work transitions improves the quality of the horse's musculoskeletal system, his impulsion, and collection, as well as his acceptance of the aids.

## WALK-HALT TRANSITION

The walk-halt transition is a good way to establish a first riding contact with a new horse. It allows you to test his "brakes and gas." It can also reveal discomfort in the horse's musculoskeletal system. When you use your leg to give the horse "gas," does the horse have impulsion or not? Is he flipping his head up? After a few strides at his natural walk, ask the horse to halt by seating deep and closing your fingers on the reins.

Is the horse rooting down on the bit, pulling the reins out of your hands?

Is he flipping his head up?

Is he overexaggerating his response?

Is he running behind the bit?

Is he relaxed when he halts?

Is he standing square?

After halting, if the horse stands square naturally, give him a pat and move on to more walking.

If your horse does not stand square, do not force it. Just walk forward another four to five steps again and repeat your halt aids. Is there an improvement? If yes, try a few more times. The repetitions will help your horse improve. If there is no improvement, make a note and keep it in mind as a potential problem.

If the horse is anxious during this exercise, do not try to back him up because he could rear and cause you to fall.

## WALK-TROT TRANSITION

The walk-trot transition is a simple transition. How your horse behaves during a walk-trot transition can indicate discomfort in his musculoskeletal system. Is your transition from walk to trot smooth?

When you ask your horse to gear up from a walk to a trot, you should feel the area of his back just behind the saddle rise beneath you as his hip flexor and extensor muscles tense up to produce forward motion. If the horse showed some weak or sore muscle at a walk, it might very well appear less pronounced at a trot. This is due to the masking effect of the muscle groups working strongly together at the faster gait. Any lameness that is still obvious at a trot could indicate that the problem lies deeper, for example, in a ligament or a joint.

Is your horse keeping his rhythm, straightness, and regularity through the transitions?

How does he accept your aids?

Is your horse responsive to your transition demands or not?

Is the walk-trot transition sluggish? This could indicate a hind end problem, either from poor training or from a musculoskeletal problem. With a young horse it could simply mean a lack of training. An older horse should know how to use himself by then, so sluggishness is not desirable; it could be a symptom of a more serious problem.

## WALK-CANTER TRANSITION

The walk-canter transition may be considered a more advanced level of work, but asking your horse to do it will tell you about his level of training. The walk-canter transition asks your horse to really gather himself and rock back. This puts a lot of pressure over the entire back and hindquarters. How does your horse behave during this walk-canter transition?

If your horse does not shift his weight behind, this could indicate some potential problems in the hindquarters, possibly the hips or the back.

How does your horse accept your aids?

Is your horse responsive to your transition demands or not?

Is your transition smooth?

Is your horse keeping his straightness through the transitions?

Is the walk-canter transition weak? With a young horse it could simply be a lack of training. An older horse should know how to use himself by then, so weakness in the hinds is not good; it could be a symptom of a musculoskeletal problem.

As an exercise, repeating the walk-canter transition improves the quality of the horse's musculoskeletal system, his impulsion, and collection as well as his acceptance of the aids.

# 11

## THE TROT

The trot, or "jog" in western discipline, is the gait that will allow you to differentiate the problems of muscular origin from deeper conditions such as ligament sprain or skeletal misalignment. Lameness when walking, due to a sore or strained muscle, might very well appear less pronounced or even completely disappear at the trot. This is due to the masking effect of the muscle groups working strongly together at this faster gait. If the lameness perceived at a walk continues at the trot, it most likely reveals a deeper problem such as a ligament sprain, a joint condition (arthritis), or a skeletal subluxation.

## THE NATURAL TROT

The horse's natural two-beat trot gait, with the horse's leg coupled in diagonal pairs, is a great gait to evaluate the horse's balance, power, and suppleness. Between the movements of each diagonal pair of legs (left hind/right front and right hind/left front), there is a moment of suspension, with all four limbs off the ground. The horse that can accomplish all the variations of the trot evenly to his left and to his right is a very well-developed athlete. However, this trot evaluation gives you a chance to see all the aspects of your horse's fitness.

The trot is very rhythmic and easy to follow. You can either sit or rise during the trot. For our purposes, please start with the rising trot before you use the sitting trot.

### THE RISING TROT

The rising trot is mostly used to warm up a horse. This trot allows the horse to stretch and strengthen his back muscles in preparation for the sitting trot.

Up                              Down

*11.1  The Rising Trot*

Allow the horse to trot at his normal gait following the same track (see figure 9.1, page 90).

After a couple of minutes, include bends and turns to loosen the side muscles of the horse's midsection. Switch to the following track, as shown in figure 11.2.

Starting at point A, move along the rail toward corner 1. Prepare before point K to gently bend your horse to the right at approximately 45 degrees until reaching a depth of 6 feet (2 meters) from the rail. Then in the flow of things, bend your horse to the left, approximately 45 degrees, until you reach the rail. Keep moving along the rail and a few feet (a meter) before point E, prepare to make another gentle bend to the right, then left as you approach H. Then prepare to make a gentle bend through the next corner (corner 2). Move along the rail to C and make an easy bend through the next corner (corner 3), then repeat the same bending exercises along the long side of the arena pass points M and F until you reach A.

Pass A and as you approach corner 1, gently bend the horse to the right and take a diagonal across the arena, through X, to corner 3. During the diagonal, switch to long reins to keep contact yet allowing your horse to relax his neck.

As you reach corner 3, bend your horse to the left, and repeat on the other rein this entire exercise all around the loop. Pass point C, corner 2, bend over point H and point K, corner 1, point A, corner 4, bend over at point F and point M, corner 3, point C, and before corner 2, gently bend your horse to the left and take a diagonal across the arena to corner 4, to reposition yourself at point A to start the next exercise.

During the trot, the horse's body should stay fairly still due to the evenness of the diagonal leg motion. Observe the following:

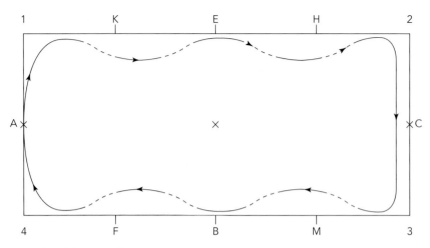

*11.2 **The Trot Suppling Exercise Diagram***

Is the horse you are trotting even in his action?

Is his rhythm smooth?

Do you feel one diagonal being stronger?

During the trot, a horse normally holds his head fairly steady. Is it the case with the horse you ride, or is his head nodding?

If sore or lame in the front legs, the horse will raise his head as the lame front leg strikes the ground. Is it the case with your horse?

If sore or lame in the hind legs, the horse will lower his head as the lame hind leg strikes the ground. Is it the case with your horse?

If the horse is sore in his neck, he will toss his neck up when you use your reins. Is it the case with your horse?

Also, during the trot, pay attention to these possibilities:

Is the horse "dishing," meaning throwing his feet outward?

Is the horse "plaiting/lacing," meaning placing one foot in front of the other due to a narrow chest?

Is the horse "brushing," due to feet turned outward, or to a hurt fetlock inside?

Is the horse "forging," where his hind feet strike his front feet?

### Variation

Riding a rising trot on the wrong diagonal will cause the horse to work harder. This variation is often used in training to muscle up the inside hind leg. You can also use it to evaluate the soundness of the hind legs.

Normally you would rise as the outside front leg is lifted. You simply need to do the opposite by sitting during the lifting of the outside front leg. Riding this way will give you a better feel of the inside hind leg. If you had already noted some discomfort with a hind leg during the walk and/or transitions, posting in opposite diagonal will be the test to verify the level of soundness in that particular leg. If there is some degree of lameness, you will feel the horse "falling in" when using that particular leg during this exercise. Practice this exercise on a figure-8 or a serpentine (see chapter 9, exercises 2 and 3).

## THE SITTING TROT

The sitting trot is a more demanding and difficult riding exercise for both the rider and the horse. As you stay seated, the horse feels more pressure over his back and midsection as well as his fore and hindquarters. Engage in a working trot, meaning with your horse on the bit, moving freely with regular and rhythmic steps.

Repeat the suppling exercise described in figure 11.2. Your horse hock action should be good, generating strong thrust from behind. As you trot, ask yourself these questions:

Is your horse still trotting evenly in his action?

Is his rhythm still smooth, or not?

Is one diagonal still stronger or not?

*11.3  The Sitting-Working Trot*

Is his head still fairly steady or not?

Is he tossing his neck up when you use your reins?

If your horse was showing some dishing, lacing, brushing, or forging at the rising trot, is he still displaying the same at the sitting trot?

## TROT VARIATIONS

After you have evaluated your horse's normal trot, try these variations in order to evaluate his ability to compress or to lengthen his stride and the outline of his body.

### THE LENGTHENED TROT

Switch to a lengthened trot to create more physical demands on your horse's musculoskeletal system.

This particular gait reaches deeper and will help reveal ligament or joint related lameness. Ask yourself:

Is your horse still trotting evenly?

Is his rhythm still smooth?

Are there any noticeable changes?

*11.4  The Lengthened Trot*

## THE COLLECTED TROT

Next, collect the trot. This will cause the horse's entire frame to compress and elevate. Your horse will lift and round his back, move his limbs higher, and work his muscles harder.

The collected trot will put additional stress and body weight on your horse's hindquarter muscles and joints. This will help you evaluate the amount of wear and tear present in his joints, if any. Keep in mind that the older the horse, the more chance of him having some form of DJD (degenerative joint disease). Note:

Are there any new changes?
How is your horse responding to you aids?
Is your horse still trotting evenly in his action?
Is his rhythm still smooth?
Is one diagonal still stronger?
Is his head still fairly steady?

*11.5  The Collected Trot*

## THE MEDIUM TROT

Progressively move to a medium trot, combining the collected effort with the lengthening of the stride.

How is the horse responding?
Are there any new changes?
Is your horse still trotting even in his action?
Is his rhythm affected?

## THE EXTENDED TROT

Finish this trot exercise cycle with an extended trot, where your horse goes all out pushing hard from behind and extending his shoulders and forelegs to the maximum while maintaining his neck and head in a frame.

*11.6  The Medium Trot*

*11.7 **The Extended Trot***

How is the horse responding?

Are there any noticeable new changes?

Is your horse still even in his action?

Is his rhythm affected?

## THE TROT LEG YIELD EXERCISE

The combination of the leg yield exercise with the velocity of the trot is a good exercise to further challenge and evaluate the suppleness of your horse musculature. This exercise will help you see if he is equally strong in both directions or if he has a dominant side. Engage in exercise 4 (see chapter 9, page 93) and follow the outline shown in figure 11.8 to verify the following:

Is your horse as supple to the left leg yield as he is to the right?

Are his steps measured and even?

Do you see his inside eye, or is his neck not bending enough? This could indicate deep muscular tension on both sides of the neck.

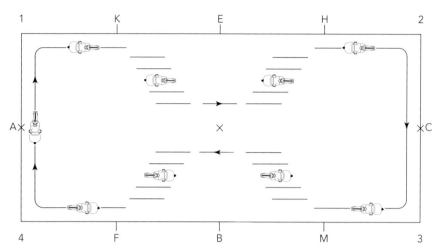

*11.8* **The Trot Leg Yield Exercise Diagram**

Is the horse crooked with his haunches moving sideways? This could indicate some lumbar or sacral discomfort. Be sure it is not caused by your inside leg being too far back.

## THE TROT SHOULDER-IN EXERCISE

Here, too, the velocity of the trot combined with the shoulder-in exercise will further challenge the suppleness of your horse's musculature. This exercise will help you better evaluate the symmetry of his body as you ride him in both directions. It will also help you determine his stronger side. Engage in exercise 5 (see chapter 9, page 95) to verify the following:

Is your horse as supple to the left shoulder-in as he is to the right shoulder-in?

Are his steps even?

Is his neck curving properly or is he uncomfortable?

Is your horse bending nicely? If not, it could indicate some lumbar or sacral discomfort. Be sure it is not caused by your inside leg being too far back.

## TROT TRANSITIONS

As with the walk transition, during the trot transitions when the horse must speed up or slow down, the horse switches gaits. Due to the velocity of the movement, the pressure on the musculoskeletal system is even greater. So, to maintain his balance during the transitions, the horse has to tighten his muscles and ligaments harder. The difficulty of execution during any of these transitions will identify the area of concern for your horse.

## TROT-WALK TRANSITION

During the trot-walk transition, the horse has to slow down his pace. How the horse behaves during this transition will reveal the soundness of his musculoskeletal system.

Is your transition from trot to walk smooth?

Does he toss his head up?

Is he sensitive in his mouth?

Does the horse trip itself behind?

Does he trip in his forehand?

Tripping reveals that the horse loses his balance in down transition. It is important to understand why. This may be due to a weakness in his musculature due to poor training, or a lack of muscle strength, or it could be due to some soreness in the skeletal and joint systems.

## TROT-HALT TRANSITION

When asking your horse to halt from his rhythmic, two-beat gait, you're asking him to brace himself. How your horse behaves during this down transition will reveal the soundness of his skeletal system.

Is your transition from trot to halt smooth?

Does your horse trip on his forehand?

Does he toss his head up?

Is he sensitive in his mouth?

Does the horse trip behind?

As mentioned with the trot-walk transition, tripping is a sign that your horse loses his balance during down transition. Most likely, his skeleton is showing some discomfort.

## TROT-CANTER TRANSITION

The trot-canter transition is a simple transition where your horse moves from a two-beat natural rhythm to a three-beat natural rhythm. He has to collect himself more over his back to provide the push-off necessary for the canter. How your horse behaves during this up transition can reveal discomfort in his musculoskeletal system.

Is your transition from trot to canter smooth?

Is he not collecting himself properly? It could be a sign of discomfort in his hock, possibly his hips or back.

Does he pull down? If the horse was already pulling down during the walk-trot transition, it really shows a lack of balance. You need to understand why. Is it because of weakness, soundness, or training? Indeed, conformation plays a role, especially if the horse has a long neck and small hinds.

Does the horse race or speed into the canter? This too reveals a balance issue, as the horse change rhythm from rocking goes from hind to front end.

Transitions from trot to canter and back to trot help loosen the horse longitudinally, contributing to his suppleness, looseness, coordination, and balance. This very particular transition is also good for building the horse's back musculature as he moves from a diagonal trot movement to a three-beat canter movement. With reasonable use, repeated transitions can improve the quality of the horse's musculoskeletal system, his impulsion, and collection, as well as his acceptance of the aids.

Indeed, the age of the horse plays a factor in his ability to perform. You can easily excuse a young untrained horse in performance issues, but an older horse should know all this. So how is your horse responding to these transitions?

If the horse does well, that tells you he is naturally balanced and fit. If he progressively gets better, that tells you he has a good mental attitude, is smart, and has natural balance. If the horse does not do well during these transitions, that tells you he has problems that can range from lack of proper training to weakness or unsoundness of the hinds, possibly the back.

# 12

## THE CANTER

The canter gait is a powerful one where the horse really pushes hard from the hindquarters to reach higher speed. This gait will give you an opportunity to really test the back, hips, and hind legs of your horse. Riding the canter at the horse's natural pace, and then its variations, will really help you determine the hindquarter's soundness, or lack thereof.

### THE NATURAL CANTER

The natural canter is an easier and more comfortable gait for the horse, producing a rolling and rocking horse feeling for the rider.

This three-beat gait has a movement of suspension where, for a short moment, all four feet are off the ground and underneath the horse's body. A horse usually uses a right lead when going to the right (clockwise) and a left lead when going to the left (counterclockwise). This allows him to better control his balance, as his leading foreleg acts as a small pivot during turning. For a horse to keep his balance during a turn at a canter is more difficult than at a trot or a walk. Cantering on a curved line on the correct lead allows the horse to be at his most balanced with the least effort.

The *canter lead*: The foreleg that touches down in the third beat of the canter determines the lead.

So here is a chronicle of the footsteps on the right lead, clockwise:

First beat: left hind
Second beat: right hind/left front (together)
Third beat: right front
Suspension: all four feet off the ground

*12.1 The Natural Canter*

And here are the chronicle footsteps on the left lead, counterclockwise:

First beat: right hind
Second beat: left hind/right front (together)
Third beat: left front
Suspension: all four feet off the ground

Keep in mind that the differences you will feel between the qualities of one lead versus the other are usually normal reflections of that horse's natural sidedness. From the walk and trot exercises, you probably already have identified which is the horse's good side and which is his difficult side. How is your horse's symmetry?

Use these differences of symmetry as indications of possible areas of weakness, stiffness, or problems. Some areas will be adjustable through strengthening exercises and hands-on massage. However, deeper-seated problems will require your veterinarian's supervision for proper diagnosis and a course of treatment.

Lateral movement exercises and counter-canter exercises will increase a horse's sense of balance and will develop strength and flexibility of his musculoskeletal system evenly on both sides. When a horse is able to counter-canter, it shows great fitness, great suppleness, and great balance.

## CANTER VARIATIONS

After you have evaluated your horse's normal canter, try the following variations to evaluate his ability to compress or to lengthen his stride and the outline of his body at this particular gait.

### THE WORKING CANTER

Start with a working canter, with your horse on the bit.

He should show balance, even strides, and a regular three-beat rhythm with good impulsion and good hock action. Ask:

Is your horse showing good hock action?

Is he dragging his hinds?

Is he lethargic, lacking impulsion, turning his canter into a four-beat gait?

When one hind leg strikes down, the other hind leg should come up and reach well under the horse's belly. Is it the case with your horse? If it is not the case, if your horse rushes his off hind leg forward, resulting

*12.2  The Working Canter*

in a quick and "heavy" canter, it might be revealing of a lack of balance. This situation can be related to:

Conformation, especially if the horse lacks angles

Soundness from the hip, stifle, and hock joints

A tight musculature, especially from the back muscles, the hamstring, and the gluteal muscle groups

Tension from the nervous system (travel, training, fatigue, and depression)

The last two points can easily be improved upon, where the first two points might not be easily dealt with.

## THE LENGTHENED CANTER

Increase the working gait by switching to a lengthened canter to demand longer strides at the same gait.

Is your horse still showing good hock action?

Is he keeping his rhythm?

*12.3 The Lengthened Canter*

## THE COLLECTED CANTER

Then move to a collected canter. This will require your horse to lower, yet be more active with his hindquarters and to raise and be lighter with his shoulders while working shorter strides.

This collected canter is more compressed and lifted than the working canter. Ask yourself:

Is you horse capable of collecting himself properly?

Do you feel some surge underneath you while his forelegs lighten?

Is your horse still showing good hock action?

Is he keeping his rhythm?

If your horse has difficulty with his collected canter, he might be experiencing some myofascial restrictions.

## THE MEDIUM CANTER

After a few strides in the collected canter, push your horse to a medium canter to amplify his strides.

*12.4 **The Collected Canter***

*12.5  **The Medium Canter***

Think of these questions as you are riding:

How is you horse responding?
Do you feel a distinct impulsion from the hindquarters?
Is your horse feeling free and balanced?
Is he keeping his rhythm?

## THE EXTENDED CANTER

Then after a few strides, switch to an extended canter. This is a canter where your horse will elongate his frame to the maximum in order to reach the utmost stride length at top speed.

How is you horse responding?
Is your horse feeling balanced?
Is he keeping his rhythm?

If the horse you are riding is balanced and fit, you should be able to go from a 16- to a 12- to a 10-foot stride without changing the rhythm. If the rhythm changes, it is a sign that the horse somehow is losing his balance due to soreness from an old injury. The compression increase

*12.6  The Extended Canter*

during collection affects the soundness of the skeletal structures. It might be revealing of an old suspensory ligament injury or possible developing arthritis.

## CANTER TRANSITIONS

Due to the speed generated during a canter, the down transitions from a canter will really put pressure on the musculoskeletal system of the horse as the horse switches gaits. He has to go from an asymmetric gait where the footfalls of the fore and hind legs occur as couplets, to a symmetrical gait where the left and right footfalls of the fore and hind legs are evenly spaced in time. To keep his balance during these down transitions, the horse has to work harder at tightening his muscles and ligaments. Problems of execution seen during these transitions will identify the area of concern for your horse.

### THE CANTER-TROT TRANSITION

How does your horse behave during down transitions?

Is your transition from canter to trot smooth?
Does his head go up? It could be discomfort in the forehand.

Does he pull down? If your horse was already pulling down during the trot-walk transition, it really shows a lack of balance. It could be revealing of discomfort in the back or hip.

Does the horse lose his straightness? This could be revealing of a back discomfort.

Is he "funny" with his hinds? It could be revealing of hind-limb problems such as in the hocks.

## CANTER-WALK TRANSITION

This canter-walk transition, slowing down your horse's pace, will increase pressure over his skeleton and joints. It will reveal quickly if there is any discomfort in his musculoskeletal system.

Is your transition from canter to walk smooth?

Does his head go up?

Does he pull down on your hand?

Does he trip himself in his forehand?

Does the horse trip himself behind?

Does he feel weak in the hinds?

Tripping during a down transition reveals that the horse loses his balance probably due either to a weakness in his musculature because of poor training or lack of muscles, or to some soreness in the skeletal and joint systems.

## CANTER-HALT TRANSITION

The abrupt switch from canter speed to full halt really challenges the horse's entire musculoskeletal system. How your horse behaves during a canter-halt transition will reveal the soundness of his body:

Is your transition from canter to halt smooth?

Does he toss his head up?

Does he pull down on your hand?

Does he trip himself in his forehand?

Does the horse trip himself behind?

If your horse can halt smoothly from a canter, this tells you he is in fine musculoskeletal condition.

# 13

## MORE ADVANCED RIDING AND JUMPING

For the more experienced riders, here are some more difficult exercises that will help you further evaluate the muscular fitness of your horse. Each person's own riding level will determine the level of execution of these exercises. However, it is important to execute these exercises with the proper signals, since the resulting evaluation will vary depending on the execution.

## THE HAUNCHES-IN (TRAVERS) EXERCISE

In this exercise, the horse's hindquarters are brought to the inside of the wall (away from the wall) while the shoulders and neck remain fairly straight on the track, as shown in figure 13.1.

The haunches-in exercise is a good test of suppleness and strength for the hindquarters, midsection, and shoulders of your horse. Think about the following:

Is your horse holding the "travers" well?

Is he steady?

Is he raising his neck?

Is he tossing his head?

Ride both sides with his haunches in for a few strides to evaluate his suppleness and strength. Compare sides and see if he is even during that movement.

*13.1 **The Haunches–in (Travers) Exercise***

# THE HAUNCHES-OUT (RENVERS) EXERCISE

This exercise is the reverse of the haunches–in, with the horse traveling in direction of the bend, with his hindquarters next to the wall. as shown in figure 13.2.

The haunches-out exercise is also a good test of suppleness and strength of your horse's hindquarters, midsection, and shoulders. Ask yourself:

Is your horse holding the "renvers" well?

Is he steady?

Is he raising his neck?

Is he tossing his head?

To see if he is even on both sides, ride him to the left and to the right with his haunches out for a few strides to compare his suppleness and strength.

*13.2 The Haunches-out (Renvers) Exercise*

## THE TURNING ON THE FOREHAND EXERCISE

In this exercise, the haunches do most of the moving and the shoulders remain almost on the spot, as shown in figure 13.3.

This is a good way to test the soundness of the hindquarters and the lower spine (lumbosacral area). Observe:

How does your horse respond to your command?

Is he equally supple going onto both the left and the right side with even steps? If not, which side is he showing difficulty with?

Is he spinning away, avoiding the bend?

## THE TURNING ON THE HAUNCHES EXERCISE

This exercise is where the forehand does most of the moving, and the haunches remain almost on the spot, as shown in figure 13.4.

*13.3  **The Turning on the Forehand Exercise***

*13.4  **The Turning on the Haunches Exercise***

This is a good way to test the soundness of the forehand and the hind end. Be aware of the following:

How does your horse respond to your command?

Is he equally supple going onto both the left and the right side with even steps? If not, which side is he showing difficulty with?

Is he spinning away, avoiding the bend?

# CAVALLETTIS AND JUMPS

Using cavallettis and jumps will also help you further evaluate the overall fitness of your horse. For the good development of this section of the program, it is important that you let the horse ride naturally. Just influence him to go forward, straight, or to turn left or right. Do not help him, support him, or dictate to him what to do. Just enjoy the ride. Let the horse relax and concentrate on the obstacle.

## CAVALLETTIS

A *cavalletti* is the name given to a single rail on the ground, usually 4 to 6 inches in diameter, either loose or mounted to a firm base. A cavalletti creates the smallest possible jump, only a few inches high. It is therefore very safe for an evaluation. Cavallettis contribute to building the confidence of horse and rider. Start first by using a grid of three to six rails, spaced every 4.5 feet on average, as shown in figure 13.5.

### Walking over Cavallettis

Cavallettis are used to teach the horse to pick up his feet and to be aware of where he puts his feet. Walk your horse over the grid of cavallettis, as shown in figure 13.6. Repeat several times, approaching the grid from the left and from the right, also going away from and toward the gate. Pay close attention to your horse's movements to see if they differ when walking toward or away from the gate, and when using a left or right approach.

During the walk, observe the following:

Is the horse picking up his feet well?

Is he even between his left and right side?

Is the horse sloppy?

Does he speed up his pace?

Does he slow down?

Is there any difference in direction (toward/away from gate)?

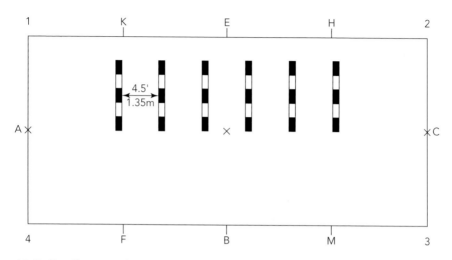

*13.5 Cavalletti Grid*

*13.6 Walking over Cavallettis*

*Trotting over Cavallettis*

Ride the same grid shown in figure 13.5 at a normal trot. Your trot should be slow yet impulsive. Keep your reins loose and stay off the horse's back, as shown in figure 13.7.

Feel and observe how the horse behaves as he approaches and negotiates the cavallettis. Ask yourself the following questions:

Is the horse balanced?

Is he lazy?

Is he sluggish?

Does he pick up his leg well?

Is he on the forehand?

Does he prefer a lead or another?

Is there a difference between a left-hand approach and a right-hand approach?

Is there a difference between going toward or away from the gate?

*13.7 **Trotting over Cavallettis***

*Jumping Cavallettis*

The next exercise will help you further challenge the balance and fitness of your horse. Change the grid pattern to include a small cross-rail jump and a straight jump, as shown in figure 13.8. Keep three rails on the floor, spaced every 4.5 feet, followed by a cross-rail jump placed at 8 or 9 feet from the last cavalletti. Depending on your horse's height, place a 2.5- to 3-feet-high fence jump at between 30 to 36 feet away from the cross-rail jump.

The cross-rail fence is one of the best jumps for this program because it is low and by its shape it invites the horse to jump in its center, as shown in figure 13.9.

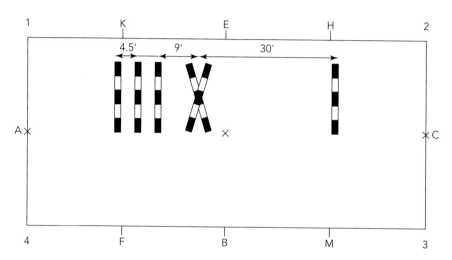

**13.8 *Cavalletti Grid with Jumps***

**13.9 *Jumping over Cross-Rails***

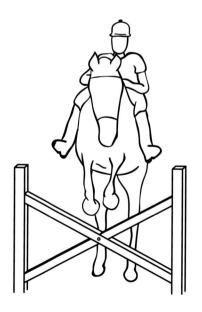

As you proceed over the cross-rail jump, ask yourself the following questions:

Is the horse using his forehand well?
Are the forelegs rising evenly?
Are his knees tight to the chest?
Is the horse using his back well?
Is the horse using his hinds well?
Does the horse crouch and jump like a cat?
Is the horse heavy in the landing?

When landing, engage in a gentle canter for three strides to jump the straight fence, as shown in figure 13.10.

Fence jumping accentuates the vertical take-off component of the jump. Go through the same set of questions asked earlier for the cross-rail jump. The way this higher level of difficulty affects your horse's jump will reveal his jumping talent, or lack thereof.

*13.10 **Jumping over a Straight Fence***

# 14

## THE REP ROUTINE

This chapter offers you safe guidelines to properly exercise your horse. Part one of the REP gives your horse time to warm up his muscles before moving to more advanced work. For the first five minutes of your program, ride your horse "long and low," meaning in a long-and-low frame, as shown in figure 14.1.

While you warm up your horse, you can proceed to your evaluation, following the information given in chapter 10. The second part helps you further warm up your horse and yet start working him. Keep the information provided in chapter 11 in your mind as you ride this second part. The third part allows you to safely push your horse a little more into work so you can go through the information presented in chapter 12. The fourth part allows you to exercise your horse in a more advanced frame, to go over cavallettis and to jump. These exercises will also give you important information as you answer the questions posed in chapter 13.

When you have completed the REP, it is equally important to ensure a cool-down period in order to avoid the stiffening of the muscles. Begin the cool-down process with a rising trot, keeping your horse's neck low so he stretches his back muscles for a few minutes. Then reduce to a walk for five minutes minimum, riding "long and low" again until your horse's breathing has calmed down.

## FIRST PART: THE WALK

Start you REP by asking your horse to walk at his normal gait. Follow the patterns shown in exercise 1, the straight lines. This is a gentle way to warm up his muscles and to begin your evaluation, as discussed in chapter 9. Continue to walk using the pattern of exercise 2, the half circles, and exercise 3, the serpentine, to further loosen his musculoskeletal system through the bending. Pay particular attention to this phase since discomfort of execution might reveal a possible problem.

*14.1 Warming Up "Long and Low"*

Then execute exercise 4, lateral work with leg yield, and exercise 5, lateral work with shoulder in, to further engage his top line and neck. Pay close attention to his performance because small details will show you where his discomfort is. Then finish this first part by asking your horse to do a walk-halt transition. Make note of all the different aptitudes of your horse, as mentioned in chapter 9.

## SECOND PART: THE TROT

From a normal walk, ask your horse to do a walk-trot transition. Pay close attention to how your horse negotiates this transition. Using a relaxed forward rising trot, go through the patterns of exercises 1 to 3. This will further loosen your horse's musculature on both sides of his body, as well as his top line and neck. Then switch to a sitting trot and engage in exercise patterns 1 to 5 in a normal trot. Then repeat at a lengthened trot, collected trot, medium trot, and extended trot. All of these variations of the trot gait will contribute to further loosening the horse while giving you precious information on your horse's fitness, as explained in chapter 11.

Conclude the second part of the REP by asking your horse to do a trot-walk transition, followed by a walk-halt transition. Pay attention to your horse's ability to downshift. Next, ask your horse to stand square, then engage in the stepping backward exercise, as described in chapter 7. Observe your horse well during that final section of the second part.

# Third Part: The Canter

Engage back into a normal walk for a few steps, then ask your horse for a walk–canter transition.

Using a natural canter, go through exercises 1 to 3. When done, repeat exercises 1 to 3, engaging in the lengthened canter, the collected canter, and the medium canter. Finish by practicing exercise 1 at the extended canter. Pay close attention to each of the variation gaits during every exercise because they will reveal much information, as explained in chapter 12.

# Fourth Part: Advanced Riding and Jumping

By now you have a pretty good feel of how your horse is moving and behaving. This fourth and last part helps you better evaluate some more advanced fitness skills from your horse. Using the pattern of exercise 1, ride the "Haunches-in (Travers)" exercise and the "Haunches-out (Renvers)" exercise. Follow with the "Turning on the Haunches" exercise and the "Turning on the Forehand" exercise.

For those interested in jumping, the cavalletti exercise is a must. Arrange the cavallettis as shown in figure 13.5 in chapter 13. First walk your horse over them, then trot him over them.

Next, rearrange the configuration, adding a couple of small jumps, as shown in figure 13.8 in chapter 13. As you proceed to jump these obstacles, pay close attention to your horse's action/reaction, as explained in chapter 13.

# Conclusion

The REP is designed to assist you in keeping your horse flexible and in minimizing any muscle tension or toxin buildup as a result of your riding. This program will not get your horse fatigued or resistant. Each exercise gently and progressively warms up your horse and prepares him for the next exercise.

Following the pattern presented in this book not only will save you time, but also will help you relax and focus on your horse and his physical and mental abilities.

I advise you to read this second section of the book thoroughly several times, before you attempt these exercises. Later on, as you practice these exercises, review the REP from time to time as you progress. It will always refresh your mind, as it is important you have a thorough understanding of each individual exercise to ensure maximum benefit during the REP.

Make notes of the various types of resistance or difficulties you notice from your horse. Any difficulty shown by your horse during the execution may reveal a possible problem. Should you have difficulty with one of the exercises, you can always do it again to ensure that what you see and/or feel is consistent. The point in this program is not to create any stress or resistance in the horse while you ride. Just concentrate on the smoothness of execution, relaxing yourself and your horse so you can flow and perform these simple exercises without creating any resistance in your horse.

To help you keep track, here is a chart to help you take notes.

## RIDING EVALUATION PROGRAM (REP)

| GAIT | VARIATION | COMMENTS |
|------|-----------|----------|
| WALK | Natural | |
| | Medium | |
| | Collected | |
| | Extended | |
| | Leg Yield | |
| | Shoulder-In | |
| | Transitions | |
| TROT | Natural | |
| | Lengthened | |
| | Collected | |
| | Medium | |
| | Extended | |
| | Leg Yield | |
| | Shoulder-In | |
| | Transitions | |

| GAIT | VARIATION | COMMENTS |
|---|---|---|
| CANTER | Natural | |
| | Working | |
| | Lengthened | |
| | Collected | |
| | Medium | |
| | Extended | |
| | Transitions | |
| ADVANCE RIDING | Haunches-In | |
| | Haunches-Out | |
| | Turning on Forehand | |
| | Turning on Haunches | |
| CAVALLETTIS | Walk | |
| | Trot | |
| | Jump Cross-rails | |
| | Jump Straight Fence | |

# PART III

# THE PALPATION EVALUATION PROGRAM (PEP)

The Palpation Evaluation Program, or PEP, is a simple and easy to carry out multipoint routine. It will allow you to check 25 important musculoskeletal points on each side of your horse. This "25-point palpation routine" gives you the opportunity to further investigate and verify your earlier findings from your REP (riding evaluation program, the second part). This hands-on PEP helps you determine what the horse's musculoskeletal system is really showing. If during your riding evaluation program you had noticed some difficulty of execution or problems, you will now be able to follow up with your own hands-on palpation and stretching to locate the problem, if any, and to call your veterinarian right away to prevent further aggravation.

Because it is easier to prevent than to recover, this PEP is an important tool. With this palpation routine, you will be able to feel and detect any abnormalities and problems much sooner than by sight. A regular application of the PEP to evaluate your horse's musculoskeletal fitness will help you detect early signs of soreness and muscular compensation that characterize the onset of possible problems. This early detection will help you make adjustment in the progression of your training program to better maintain your horse's good fitness and performance. At the same time, the PEP will keep you alert to more serious conditions, allowing you to call your veterinarian right away and prevent further aggravation. Regular application of the PEP will save you time and money in the long run, not to mention the increased bond with and appreciation of your horse.

The valuable information contained in this third part will give you the skills that will make you comfortable in carrying out this PEP.

Keep in mind that when performing the PEP on a young horse, he might not always relate right away to your demands because of his inexperience. Be patient and stay calm. Smile and praise the horse to build up his confidence. Especially when grabbing his limb, you might worry or scare him. Take the time to comfort him. Make him feel safe with your caresses and your soft voice. A few minutes of comforting will build his trust in you and interest him in what you want of him. Do not rush through this early connection, since it will influence the rest of your relationship.

# 15

In this chapter you can see the outline of the 25 points that make up the palpation evaluation program (PEP) of your horse's musculoskeletal system. The feedback perceived during your application of this PEP will give you a realistic picture of the actual fitness of your horse.

The precise information offered in these chapters will make you comfortable to palpate the 25 most important musculoskeletal points on each side of your horse. Here is the outline of the PEP:

1. The teeth and mandible
2. The temporomandibular joint (TMJ)
3. The occipital bone of the skull and the first cervical vertebra area (C0-C1)
4. The second to fifth cervical vertebrae area (C2-C3-C4-C5)
5. The sixth and seventh cervical vertebrae (C6-C7)
6. The withers (thoracic spinous processes, T5-T11)
7. The back (thoracic spine)
8. The rib cage
9. The lower back (lumbar spine)
10. The sacrum
11. The tail
12. The hip
13. The scapula and its muscle sling
14. The point of shoulder
15. The elbow joint
16. The knee joint
17. The canon bone, suspensory ligament, and flexor tendon
18. The fetlock joint

19. The pasterns and hoof
20. The coxofemoral (hip) joint
21. The stifle joint
22. The hock joint
23. The suspensory ligament and flexor tendon
24. The fetlock
25. The pasterns and hoof

For your convenience, the information concerning the 25 points is presented in four sections:

1. Chapter 16: The head and neck, points 1 to 5
2. Chapter 17: The withers, back, sacrum, and tail, points 6 to 12
3. Chapter 18: The forelimb, points 13 to 19
4. Chapter 19: The hind limb, points 20 to 25

In order to get a true "reading" of the actual horse's physical condition, it is important to carry out the entire palpation evaluation program. Everything is interconnected, meaning that a problem in a particular muscle group can correspond directly to a local problem, or it can be part of a compensation phenomenon for another problem located somewhere else. As you proceed with your PEP, keep in mind the horse's conformation, predisposition, and the discipline he is involved in, because these factors are a strong influence on his overall fitness.

*15.1 The 25-Point Palpation Evaluation Program Outline*

This palpation evaluation program is done in a very gentle manner, so that the horse enjoys the entire process. The TLC (tender loving care) that you will give him during your application of this routine will make him more compliant and more giving.

# Early Practice

In the beginning, it is to your advantage to practice on a horse you know well. During your learning process, the patience of a friendly horse will be working to your advantage. However, it will not be long before you absorb the material presented here, and feel comfortable in applying the PEP onto any horses, anywhere and at anytime. This knowledge will stay with you for the rest of your life.

# Recommendations about the PEP

Here are some important pointers that will save you time and facilitate your work.

## Patience

Be gentle and have patience with your horse as you proceed through each step of this program. You have more to gain by tuning in to your horse, by interesting and inviting him to do things for you, than by forcing him to comply. If your horse refuses to do something, do not insist at that moment. Refusal is usually a sign that the horse is not comfortable, that there is a physical cause that creates pain or potential for pain. Be patient. Consider moving on to another part for a while, and later come back. If the horse complies then, great. If he still refuses, you might be dealing with a more serious problem.

Remember, there is a reason for everything. Sometimes it takes time to determine the reason why your horse is doing a certain thing or not doing it, but the knowledge you will gain from this book will help you make an educated guess, giving you clues on how to check and resolve these problems. Be grounded. One of your first goals is to communicate to your horse that you want to have a peaceful relationship with him, not a dominating one, a relationship based on mutual respect.

## Praising

As you work around the horse, use a lot of praising and smile as much as possible to him. Pet him with a soft touch. Make him feel special. Every time the horse does what you want, tell him right away he did the right thing. Tell him you appreciate his effort, his good work, and his cooperation. Be generous with your praising throughout your entire PEP.

## Treats

Giving the horse a treat is a great way to reward him. That will really impress him and make him feel special. Most good-tempered horses will enjoy this "reward" system, making them even more cooperative. However, be aware that a few horses with strong characters might become demanding and mouthy as they "crave" the treats. This might in someway interfere with the good development of your PEP. If you are working on a new horse, check with the owner first. You do not want to use "sweets" with a horse that has diabetes.

Also, be mindful of your word association when rewarding the horse with treats. You don't want to develop an association of expectation every time you use that word. For example, when giving a treat, if you use the phrase "good boy" or "good girl," your horse might associate that with treats. So next time you praise with the same phrase, he might stop whatever he is doing and wait for his treat!

## Choosing a Location

When performing the PEP it is important to choose a location best suited for the horse's temperament, ensuring as little traffic and disturbance as possible. Keep small pets away. Avoid loud noises as much as possible. Stay away from distractions or challenges.

Choose an area where you have plenty of space to move around. Ensure that you have enough room so you can stretch the horse comfortably. Avoid crowded spaces.

If no one else is around to assist you to hold the horse, you can use the crossties, or simply tie the horse to a pole or fence. However, it is more desirable to have somebody friendly hold the horse.

Performing the PEP on a flat and even surface will be an advantage. It will help for a better reading of the symmetry of the anatomical features, especially when looking at the legs, thorax, and hips. A wash stall at a quiet time of the day works very well for a PEP.

## Positioning the Horse

Before starting your palpation evaluation, ensure your horse stands square, with both his rear pasterns vertical from the hocks to the fetlocks. This particular stand will give you the best reading of the horse musculoskeletal structure, especially when done on a flat surface for best results.

### Asking for a Leg

Whenever asking the horse to pick up his leg, please be gentle. The first time you ask, use a gentle squeeze of the flexor tendon just above the fetlock. If your horse responds right away, great, follow with praise and move on with your palpation.

If he does not respond, ask again nicely with a little more tone in your voice and squeezing the flexor tendon in the same location a little more strongly. If he responds, great; follow with praise.

If the horse ignores you still, consider a "call to action" with a gentle yet firm hand tap over his belly to "wake him up" and gently ask for the leg again. As soon as he complies, follow with praise.

## THE HORSE'S FEEDBACK

For the smooth evolution of your work, it is important to accurately read the "feedback signs" given by your horse during your application of the PEP. Any signs of pain or discomfort given by your horse should always be considered as a warning signal, therefore learn to recognize them and pay attention.

Sure signs of apprehension are:

Eyes widening and becoming intense
A quick raising or turning the head toward you
Ears pulled back
Skin twitching or flinching
Fidgeting, tensing up

*15.2 Horse Relaxed (A)/Tense (B)*

A

B

Moving away from the pressure or swinging of the rear toward you

Tail swishing, stamping of feet

Breathing short and hard

Biting

Sudden jolts or tensing during the session can indicate that the pressure you are applying is too strong, or you are working a significant tender spot. It could be also a little bit of both.

Sometimes your horse is simply afraid of what you are doing because it might be new to him. Use a calming voice to ease his anxiety. If necessary, delay your work until your horse is in a better frame of mind. You do not want to create a worse situation by "forcing" the issue.

Sure signs of relaxation are:

Eyes half closed

Head down

Ears relaxed and to the side

Heavy sighs

Relaxing of the lower lip, nuzzling

Relaxing a hind leg

"Dropping," usually seen right after the relaxation massage routine

Monitor your horse's body language constantly and adjust your work accordingly. To be aware of the feedback signs of your horse at all times should be part of your "horse sense."

## TOUCH-SHYNESS

Some horses will show anxiety during your palpation evaluation. This can be due to what is known as *touch-shyness*. The reason for this condition may vary greatly in origin, ranging from poor handling at a young age to trauma from "irresponsible" handling. In most cases, touch-shyness over a particular area of the body indicates an underlying condition. Make sure that no contraindication applies (see "Contraindications" later in this chapter).

When touching a new horse, take the time to observe the horse's temperament and character in order to maximize your connection at the beginning of the PEP session. Most horses respond very positively. Young horses may engage in playful nabbing and nuzzling with your hands during the session. Occasionally you might run into a horse who has a strong aversion to your work on one particular site of his body, due to an emotional associated memory. Be aware, and consider temporarily backing off from working that particular area and go on working a more "positive" body part until the horse realizes the nature and the feel-good sensations associated with this work.

## PEP Application: Before or after Exercising?

Conducting a palpation evaluation before the horse is exercised will show you how the horse really is after a long rest period. This particular approach will help you better identify the areas of tension and patterns of compensation. Be aware that in this scenario, the horse will be rested and ready to go out, especially if his friends are already out. He might be restless and less accepting of your work.

To carry out a palpation evaluation after the horse has been exercised, when he is tired, calmer, and more accepting of your work is a lot easier. Also, since the structures are well warmed up and the muscles are suppler, it allows you to palpate deeper in an easier manner. However, the exercise might have erased some of the compensatory muscle tension seen with problem such as arthritis of the neck, back, or legs, or minor strains (tendon pull) and sprains (ligament pull).

With your own horse you can use both approaches at your convenience. If you meet a horse for the first time, my recommendation to you is to carry your first palpation evaluation after the horse has been exercised. In this way your very first meeting will happen with maximum safety for the both of you. If you realize this horse is a good prospect for you, you can come back for a second palpation evaluation, this time early in the morning before the horse is exercised.

## Time Factor

Carrying out a thorough palpation evaluation can take from fifteen to thirty minutes. The compliance of the horse, the physical condition of his musculoskeletal system, and your ability to carry out the PEP will be determinant factors. With practice, you will secure a good approach and sharpen your technique. This will shorten the time of your session considerably.

In less than ten minutes, you can proceed with the short relaxation massage routine and the first pass (see below) to check the key areas of the horse's musculoskeletal structures in order to ensure their overall fitness. Then you can decide if you wish to continue to a more in-depth evaluation with the second pass. Depending upon the nature of the possible problems you may find during your session, the time frame of your evaluation might expend considerably.

By observing the guidelines and recommendations mentioned earlier, you will save yourself some precious time and gain the cooperation of the horse, making this experience pleasant for all involved.

From my years of using the PEP, I recommend that you break it down into two passes. This particular approach will save you time in the long run.

*First pass:* Proceed to check the upper neck, the withers, and the sacrum, as shown in figure 15.3.

These three locations are very important musculoskeletal areas of the horse. Signs of muscle tension and/or soreness in anyone of these three areas would reveal a great deal.

For example, muscle tension, possibly soreness, and/or imbalance in the upper cervical area can be the result of compensation for a shoulder or back problem or simply related to a dental and/or TMJ issue. Tightness on either side of the withers can indicate compensatory tension for the neck or the back or simply a shoulder/leg issue. Strong muscle tension and soreness along the left side of the sacrum can indicate some sacroiliac issue. In that case your horse needs some veterinary chiropractic supervision. If these three key areas are problem free, that is good news.

*Second pass:* Proceed to check all other points of the PEP over the lower neck, the thorax, and forelimbs and hindquarters as shown in figure 15.1.

*15.3 **The Palpation Evaluation Program, First Pass Outline***

# CONTRAINDICATIONS

Contraindications refer to the specific situations in which you should *not* carry out the PEP on a horse, but instead you should consult your veterinarian.

- ❖ When your horse has a temperature over 102 degrees F (39 degrees C). A horse's regular temperature is 100 degrees F (38 degrees C). An increase in temperature occurs during serious illnesses. Feverish conditions necessitate complete rest. In that case, consult your veterinarian.
- ❖ When your horse is suffering from shock.
- ❖ When there is an open (broken skin) or healing wound (bleeding).
- ❖ When there is an acute trauma such as a torn muscle, or an area with internal bleeding such as an acute hematoma following a strong blow or sprain. Instead, use ice for the first few hours.
- ❖ Severe forms of functional nervous diseases (tetanus).
- ❖ Acute nerve problems or nerve irritation (neuralgia) in a particular area (following a wound or a bad stretch).
- ❖ During colitis, diarrhea, pregnancy, or hernias, use just a light stroking on the abdomen, and only if the horse does not mind.
- ❖ Acute arthritis that is too painful to permit stretching; this could worsen the inflammation. Instead, use cold hydrotherapy locally.
- ❖ Inflammatory conditions such as phlebitis. Use cold hydrotherapy and check with your veterinarian.
- ❖ Tumors and cysts of cancerous origin are contraindicated. Avoid the affected areas, but you may check the rest of the body. Contact a veterinarian.

Be careful when dealing with what appears to be an abnormal situation, especially if undiagnosed symptoms arise. When in doubt, contact a veterinarian for a thorough examination.

# 16

## THE HEAD AND NECK: POINTS 1 TO 5

The head and neck play an important role in the horse's movements. A horse uses his head and neck constantly to balance the rest of his body. This is obvious during the canter: the downward swing of the head will help lift the rear legs off the ground as the horse moves forward. The trot puts a tremendous amount of strain on the entire musculoskeletal system of the head and neck, as well as the rest of the body. Therefore good flexibility of both the head and neck is vital to performance. Please take a moment to review figures 5.5, 5.8, 5.9, 5.12, 5.13, and 5.15 in chapter 5 to refresh your memory of the actual location of the bones, ligaments, and muscles.

The length of the neck varies from breed to breed. Both ends of the cervical spine are subject to a lot of physical stress, and as age sets in they can be subject to arthritic degeneration.

Common problem such as regular head shaking, especially during exercises, the horse avoiding the contact with the bit, the horse playing with his tongue (tongue lolling), biting, excessive salivation, loss of appetite, and sometimes poor body condition and riding difficulties can be traced to some problem with the head and/or neck.

Conducting a massage palpation evaluation of points 1 to 5 over the head and neck will enable you to determine some very important components of the horse's health and performance, such as:

The state of his dentition: Healthy teeth are important to good assimilation of food.

The state of his temporomandibular joints (TMJs): Healthy TMJs are crucial for good contact at the bit; otherwise it will affect the quality of your riding.

The alignment of the transverse processes of each cervical vertebra throughout the entire neck: Any misalignment and/or abnormal muscular tension can indicate potentially serious musculoskeletal issues.

The presence of potential stress points in the neck musculature.

This information will help you better understand where your horse carries his stress and why.

When connecting with a young horse, due to his inexperience he might not always comply with your demands. Be patient and remain calm, smiling and praising him to build up his confidence. Do not rush. Comfort him and make him feel safe. Use a lot of soft caresses and a soft voice to praise him. These few minutes spent comforting him will create a bond of trust between you, yielding to his acceptance of your work.

# POINT 1: DENTAL EXAMINATION

A quick look at the horse's front teeth can reveal several important factors, such as bruxism (grinding the teeth), faulty teeth, and possibly a temporomandibular joint (TMJ) dysfunction. (For a quick review of the horse's dental structure, see chapter 5, page 42). Good teeth are essential to the horse for proper mastication and assimilation of his food. Poor teeth can lead not only to bad nutrition, weight loss, and digestive problems, but also to soreness in the temporomandibular joints. When a horse is sore in his TMJs, it affects his contact with the bit as well as his overall balance at any gait.

Checking the horse's teeth will give you precious information on the following:

The state of health of the horse's teeth

The alignment of the mandible with the maxilla

The condition of both temporomandibular joints

The tension present in the muscles and fasciae layers of the face

The level of inflammation present in these structures, if any

Start by examining the incisive teeth and their gum lines. Gently open the lips of the horse's mouth, as shown in figure 16.1.

When the mandible is properly positioned, the gum lines between the upper and lower incisor teeth are aligned. This is a sign of healthy teeth and TMJs. If the gum lines are not aligned, the direction of the deviation indicates the tighter TMJ side. So, for example, if the lower jaw pulls to the left, this reveals a tight left TMJ.

If your horse shows a slight deviation of the lower mandible, you need to take a closer look at his teeth. To do so, consider this technique: introduce the fingers of one of your hands to the horse's mouth at the level of the interdental space, right behind the canine teeth, as shown in figure 16.2. This will cause him to open his mouth wider.

*16.1* **Checking Incisor Teeth Alignment**

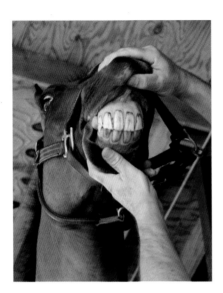

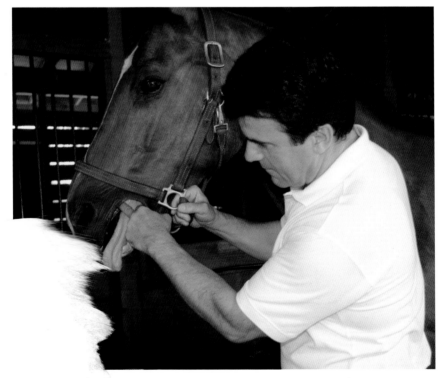

*...eeth, Opening Mouth*

Then, with your other hand, grasp his tongue firmly and bring it laterally to the other side, as shown in figure 16.3. With a little practice you will be able to introduce one hand into one side, grasp the tongue, and pull it laterally to that same side. This will prevent the horse from biting in case he resists the examination.

Look inside the mouth to examine the shape of both the premolars (the first three teeth) and the molars (the last three teeth) of the dental arcade. Take a good look at the structure of their occlusal surfaces and at the length and direction of every tooth, as shown in figure 16.4.

You can also use your free hand to palpate the edges of those teeth and feel for sharp edges or "hooks" on that one side, as shown in figure 16.5.

Then change the grasp of the tongue to the other side in order to examine the other row of teeth.

If you do not feel comfortable with this technique, or if the horse resents this approach, there is another way to evaluate the horse's teeth. Although it is not as revealing as the first technique, it will give you a good first evaluation. We know that the maxillary teeth overlap the mandible teeth. So simply pass your fingertips over the cheeks, on the ventral aspect of the maxilla's teeth, as shown in figure 16.6. This will get you a first idea if there are any faulty or broken teeth.

If your evaluation indicates that your horse's teeth are not quite right, contact your veterinarian or equine dentist right away for a proper diagnosis and course of action.

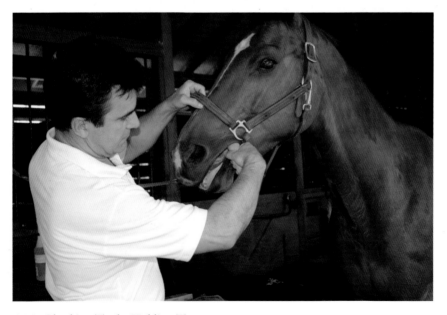

*16.3  Checking Teeth, Holding Tongue*

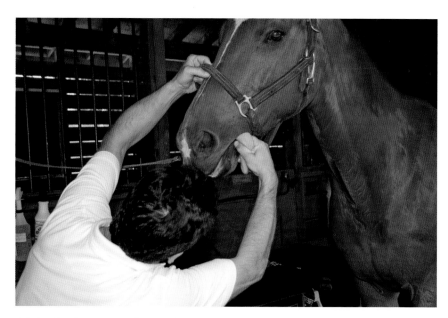

*16.4 Checking Premolars and Molars*

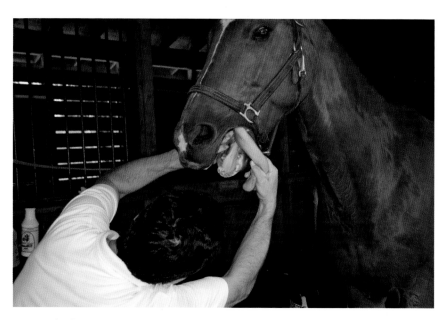

*16.5 Checking Teeth with Free Hand*

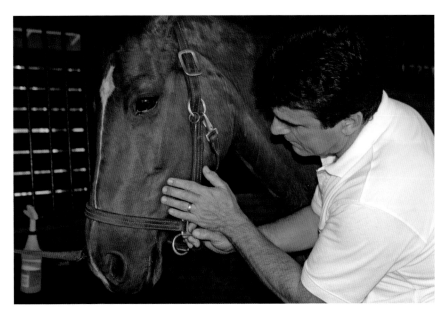

*16.6  **Checking Teeth Externally***

# POINT 2: THE TEMPOROMANDIBULAR JOINT (TMJ)

Checking the horse's TMJ will give you vital information on the following:

The state of health of the horse's TMJs

The tension present in the muscles and fasciae layers of the face

The level of inflammation in these structures, if any

Proceed to palpate the TMJ joint on each side. Starting on the left, place your right fingers in front and slightly below the left auditory canal of the ear (do not place your fingers in the auditory canal). With your other hand, introduce your left fingers over his left bars, as shown in figure 16.7. This will gently force your horse to open and close his jaw.

The opening action of the jaw should happen smoothly. If during your palpation you feel and/or even hear a small "click," this is a sure sign of joint restriction and muscle tension. Duplicate the same procedure over the right side. You should be able to tell if the jaw is opening evenly. If there is some restriction on one side, you need to investigate further.

Next, proceed to "rock the mandible." Place one hand over the ridge of the nose and hold sturdily. With your other hand, grab the lower mandible delicately and gently rock it back and forth a few times, as shown in figure 16.8. This will loosen the TMJs. If the mandible travels equally on both sides, it is a good sign. If one side is restricted, it is usually the side with the tight TMJ.

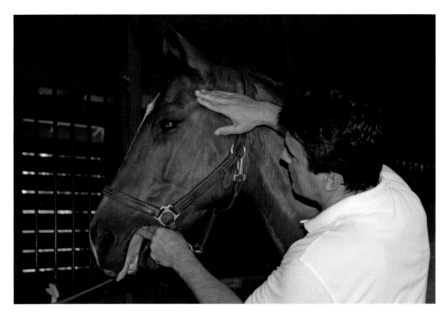

*16.7 Checking the TMJ*

## CHECKING THE OPENING OF THE MOUTH

Standing in front of the horse's mouth, gently place your thumbs on the bars of the maxilla. Then push progressively in a caudal and dorsal way to gently force the horse to open his mouth. As shown in figure 16.9, place your right thumb on the horse's left maxilla bar while pushing with your left thumb on the horse's right mandible bar to the horse's left. This will stretch the horse's right TMJ.

Next, as shown in figure 16.10, place your left thumb on the horse's right maxilla bar while pushing with your right thumb on the horse's left mandible bar to the horse's right. This will stretch the horse's left TMJ.

Observe carefully the opening of the mandible. See if it opens evenly on both sides, or if one side is tighter than the other.

If the jaw is moving unevenly to one side, if there is some heat and potentially some swelling over the TMJs, and if you feel some hyper-tonicity or some trigger points in the mastication muscles (masseter, temporalis, and occipitomandibularis, just to name the most superficial muscles), those are sure signs and symptoms of equine temporomandibu-lar dysfunction syndrome (ETDS). ETDS is a serious condition that requires veterinary and dental supervision. Massage can help a lot during recovery of ETDS. Please refer to the book *Equine Temporomandibular Dysfunction Syndrome (ETDS)* by this same author, available through the Massage Awareness library at www.massageawareness.com.

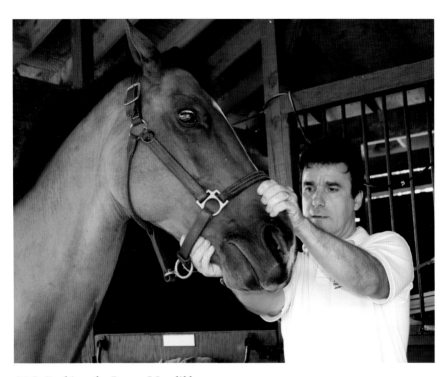

*16.8  Rocking the Lower Mandible*

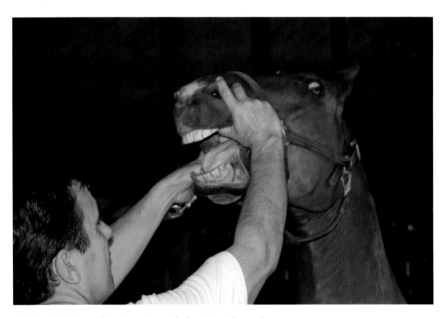

*16.9  Checking the Opening of the Mouth, Left*

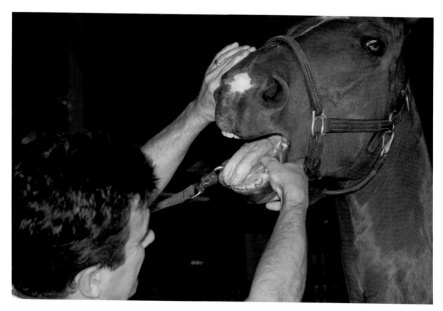

16.10 *Checking the Opening of the Mouth, Right*

# POINT 3: THE UPPER NECK

Many muscle groups and fascia layers come to attach on the first cervical vertebra and the back of the skull. Checking the upper neck will give you vital information on the following:

  The alignment of the first cervical vertebra (C1) in relationship to the skull

  The amount of muscular and fascia tension on either side of the neck

  The level of inflammation in these structures, if any

## PALPATING THE UPPER NECK

To best palpate the first cervical vertebra, position yourself in the following manner: begin by standing to the side of the horse, and gently stroke the side of his neck with your hands. Speak to the horse with a soft voice. Then come to position your head right under his mandible, as shown in illustration 16.11. Be gentle as you make contact with his mandible. Simultaneously move both your hands over the lateral aspect of the transverse processes of C1 on either side.

With your fingers, evaluate the space between the transverse processes of C1 and the ramus of the mandible. With most horses you will be able to easily set two fingers in that space. However depending on the horse breed and genetic heritage, this space might be wider, allowing you to place three fingers, or it might be narrower, allowing you to barely set one finger. This size difference is normal.

What is important is to check the evenness of the spaces on each side of the neck. If the first cervical vertebra is rotated to one side, the space between the transverse process of C1 and the mandible on that side will be narrower than the same space on the other side of the neck.

### Findings

Hopefully, you will find an evenly seated first cervical vertebra in relation to the mandible. That is a good sign, indeed; however, if your fingers perceive strong muscle tension, tenderness in reaction to your touch, and inflammatory symptoms on both sides of C1, possibly down to C2, it could be a sign of arthritis in that area. It could also possibly be a sign of compensation for a TMJ problem. In such cases you should contact your veterinarian for proper diagnosis and course of treatment.

If you detect unevenness in the space between the transverse processes of C1 and the mandible, the associated symptoms will be proportional to the degree of rotational displacement. There will be a lot of discomfort in the adjacent muscle and fascia layers on both sides of the neck upon your touch. Muscles, ligaments, and fascia tissue will be contracted on the narrow side of C1 and will be overstretched on the other, wider side of C1.

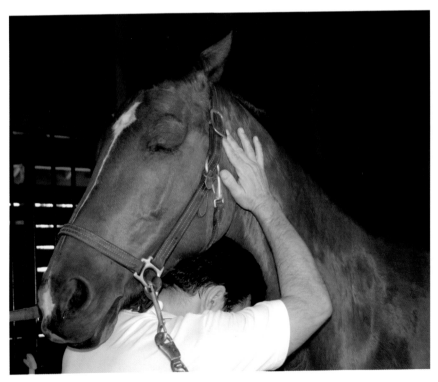

*16.11 Proper Positioning to Palpate C0-C1*

If the rotation of C1 is minimal, the symptoms might be light, showing mostly some muscle and fascia tension by the occipital bone and the first cervical vertebra. If the rotation is more severe, symptoms might include strong muscle and fascia tension, and possibly heat and mild swelling, not to mention acute pain to touch. The fascia might radiate tightness and soreness upward right up to the TMJs on both sides and downward to the lower neck. It is not uncommon to see stress points forming in adjacent muscles. Check for stress points SP1-2-3-4 (see chapter 5, pages 59–61).

A misaligned first cervical vertebra can easily be adjusted by a veterinarian chiropractor. However, for the purpose of your massage palpation evaluation, it is important for you to figure out if this rotated C1 is an isolated problem or if it is secondary (compensatory) to another more serious problem, such as a TMJ dysfunction syndrome or simply sore withers or even a sore hip.

## POINT 4: THE MIDNECK

Checking the midneck will give you precious information on the following:

The alignment of the cervical vertebrae (C 2-3-4-5)

The amount of muscular tension present in the muscles that attach to the midneck

The tension present in the fascia layers of this section of the neck

The level of inflammation in these structures, if any

### PALPATING THE MIDNECK

From the same position used to evaluate point 3, gently move both your hands simultaneously down the neck, going over the transverse processes of C2, C3, C4, and C5, as shown in figure 16.12.

Let your fingertips (see the four T's, chapter 1, page 3) give you direct feedback on the evenness of the transverse processes alignments and on the quality of the muscle and fascia tissue attaching to these vertebrae.

### Findings

If your fingers perceive strong muscle tension, tenderness, and inflammatory symptoms by C3, C4, and C5, it could be an early sign of a possible cervical static stenosis of the spine, a serious condition that requires veterinary supervision. A horse that has cervical stenosis will be sore during ventral flexion and thus will always avoid that action. Usually the compression of the spine seen in a serious case of cervical static stenosis will affect the horse's gait, both on his fore and hind legs.

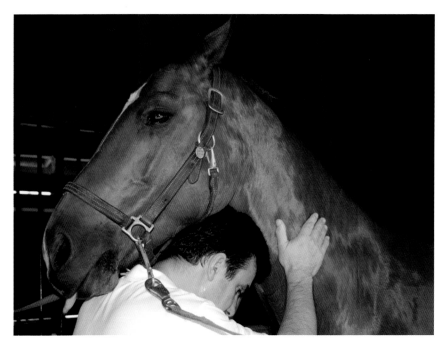

*16.12 Checking the Midneck Cervical Vertebrae*

Any misaligned midcervical vertebrae can be adjusted by a veterinarian chiropractor. For the purpose of your massage PEP, it is important for you to figure out if this particular misalignment is an isolated problem or if it is a compensatory phenomenon, secondary to another more serious problem.

## POINT 5: THE LOWER NECK

Checking the lower neck will give you information on the following:

The alignment of the last two cervical vertebrae (C6–C7) and the first rib

The amount of muscular tension present in the muscles that attach to the lower neck

The tension in the lower neck fascia layers

The level of inflammation in these structures, if any

There is a considerable amount of lateral and vertical flexibility by the six and seventh cervical vertebra. This allows the horse to bend his entire neck in any direction. This lower neck flexibility is important: it contributes to the horse's finesse in adjusting his neck as a balancer for the different strides. This lower neck flexibility is put to the test during the piaffe/passage exercises seen in dressage where the horse sustains a high head carriage while performing high leg extension for short strides.

## PALPATING THE LOWER NECK

From the same position used to evaluate the upper neck and the mid-neck, simply keep moving both your hands simultaneously and gently down the lower neck, as shown in figure 16.13.

The transverse processes of C6 and C7 are not as palpable as the prior vertebrae due to the proximity of the scapula and the thicker layers of muscles in that direct area. Let your fingers' four T's give you direct feedback on the evenness of the transverse processes' alignments and on the quality of both muscle and fascia tissues attaching to these two vertebrae.

The last cervical vertebra (C7) and the first thoracic vertebra (T1) are sometimes an area of concern. Occasionally, the head of the first rib sticks out of its socket. This condition can radiate soreness over the lower neck and the entire foreleg on the same side. Humans experience a similar condition known as thoracic outlet syndrome.

### Findings

If your fingers perceive strong muscle tension, tenderness, and inflammatory symptoms on both sides of C6 and especially C7, it could be a sign of arthritis in that area. If these symptoms are only pronounced on one side, it could indicate a rib misalignment. If your palpation of the midneck had already revealed strong muscle tension and possibly some inflammation symptoms, suspect a case of stenosis, a serious condition in which the spinal cord is compressed within the vertebral canal. In such

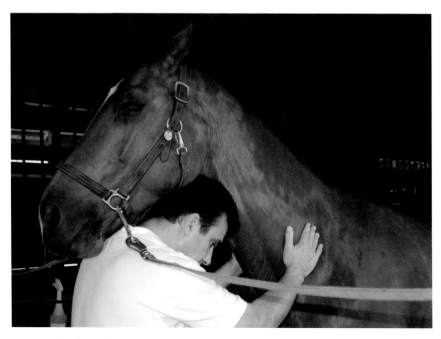

*16.13 Checking the Lower Neck Cervical Vertebrae*

a case, the horse would resist performing a ventral flexion, so offering him a carrot stretch down between his front legs will help you confirm that fact right away. If he can perform this stretch without difficulty, there is no stenosis. If he cannot stretch in that manner, it is a sign of possible stenosis. You should contact your veterinarian immediately.

A misaligned lower cervical vertebra or rib can easily be adjusted by a veterinarian chiropractor. However, for the purpose of your massage palpation evaluation, it is important for you to figure out the origin of this problem.

## ASSOCIATED STRESS POINTS OF THE NECK

Following the palpation of the skeletal features of the neck, proceed to supervise the following muscle locations for potential stress points. (For better visualization refer to the stress point location chart in chapter 5, pages 59–61.) After warming up the neck with the SEW approach (see chapter 2), use gentle kneading massage movements to work the various muscles of the neck. Use effleurage massage movement regularly, every ten seconds or so, to drain the area toward the heart. Consider using stroking massage movements to flow from one point to the other.

SP1 is found close to the third cervical vertebra, by the origin tendon of the *rectus capitis ventralis muscle*, located in the deep layer, as shown in figure 16.14.

SP2 is found close to the base of the skull, by the insertion tendon of the *splenius cervicis muscle*, located in the superficial layer, as shown in figure 16.15.

SP3 is found a few inches above the point of shoulder, three–quarters of the way down the *brachiocephalic muscle*, located in the superficial layer, as shown in figure 16.16.

SP4 is found by the middle of the anterior edge of the scapula (shoulder blade), close to the insertion tendon of the *sternothyrohyoid* and *omohyoid muscles*, both located in the deep layer, as shown in figure 16.17.

## STRETCHING THE NECK

Stretching the neck of your horse will reveal its flexibility or lack thereof. Please review figures 4.16 through 4.20 in chapter 4 for details on the various neck stretches you can perform with your animal. If your horse can perform all those stretches smoothly and evenly on each side, it means that his neck structures are fine.

If your horse appears restricted in performing a stretch to one side, it can simply indicate some muscle tension on the opposite side of the neck, limiting the depth of the stretch. It can also reveal that the horse's neck vertebrae are not properly aligned and the stretch to that side is causing some pinching and discomfort, resulting in a limited stretch. In such case, it is important to contact a veterinarian chiropractor to adjust the neck.

*16.14  Checking SP1*

*16.15  Checking SP2*

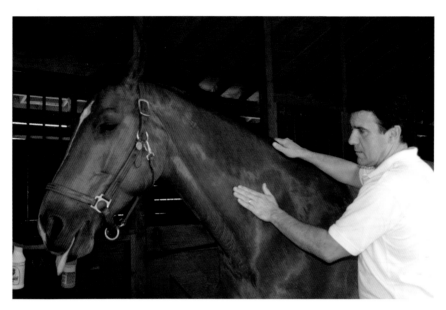

*16.16  Checking SP3*

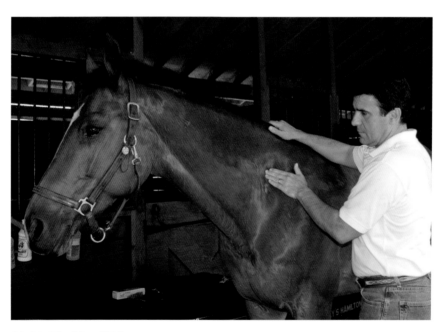

*16.17  Checking SP4*

# 17

The back is a strong structure that acts as a bridge transferring the moving power coming from the strong hindquarters onto the shoulders and neck. Adding weight on the horse (tack, saddle, and rider) is the cause of a lot of problems affecting the back structures, especially at high speed, over jumps, or during quick starts and stops. And there can be inherited structural deformities such as sway back, scoliosis, and kissing spines, all of which can affect the spine quite dramatically. Please take a moment to review figures 5.5, 5.8, 5.9, 5.12, 5.13, and 5.15 in chapter 5 of this book to refresh your memory of the actual location of these bones, ligaments, and muscles.

Good flexibility of the back is vital to good performance. If any discomfort arises in any one of the horse's limbs, the back structure will quickly compensate to absorb the difference and maintain maximum straightness and efficiency. Your massage palpation evaluation will allow you to identify areas of soreness and possibly inflammation along the various vertebrae of the back.

By conducting a massage palpation evaluation of points 6 to 12 over the head and neck you will be able to determine some very important components of the horse's health and performance, such as:

The alignment of the transverse processes of the thoracic and lumbar vertebrae throughout the entire back: Any misalignment and/or abnormal muscular tension indicates serious musculoskeletal issues.

The alignment of the ribs as they contribute to good movement

The state of the sacrum in relation to the hip

The state of the hip in relation to the back and hind limbs

The presence of potential stress points in the back musculature

The tension in the local fascia layers

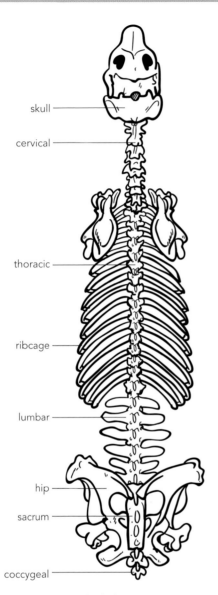

*17.1* **The Spinal Skeleton**

This information will help you better understand where your horse carries his stress and why.

## POINT 6: THE WITHERS

The withers portion of the thoracic spine (T1 to T11) is a very strong part of the horse's anatomy, since it is the cross axis between the longitudinal axis of the spine and the transverse axis of both shoulders. Onto either side, the withers attach the scapular muscle girdles as well as the neck and back extensor muscle groups. Poor alignment of the early thoracic vertebrae that make up the withers can lead to poor movement in the foreleg.

When adding the weight of the rider with saddle, undue tightness in the withers musculature will quickly become aggravated and affect the horse's locomotion, especially for horses who jump.

Poor alignment can also cause soreness when girthing up a horse with inflammation of the back muscles.

Checking the withers with your palpation skills will give you precise and precious information on the following:

The alignment of the thoracic vertebrae involved in the withers (T1 to T11)

The amount of muscular tension attaching to the withers

The tension in the local fascia layers

The level of inflammation in this structure, if any

Position yourself on the side of the horse and anchor your fingers on the opposite side of the withers as shown in figure 17.2.

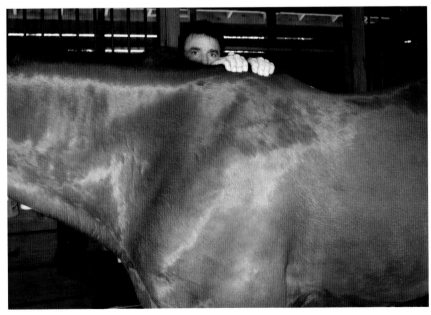

*17.2 Anchoring Fingers onto the Withers*

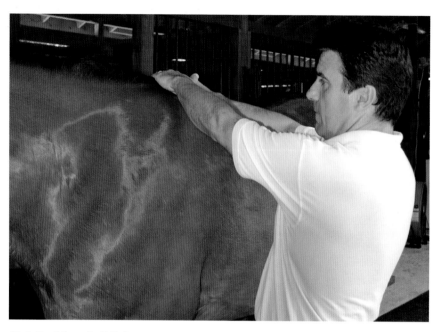

*17.3 Rocking the Withers*

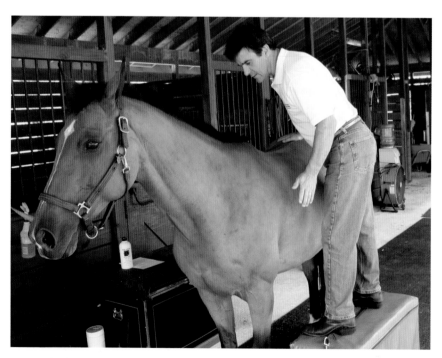

*17.4 Checking the Withers from Above*

Slowly and gently start grabbing the spinous processes that form the withers towards you, and then release them, creating a gentle rocking motion as shown in figure 17.3. Repeat six to ten times.

As you proceed, pay close attention to the sensation you feel under your fingers. Each spinous process should feel independent from the adjacent one. That accounts for healthy withers. Occasionally, you might get the sensation that two or more thoracic spinous processes are stuck together. This is a sure sign of stiffness. Repeat the same procedure from the other side and compare your sensations.

You might feel that the tension is more obvious on one side, with some of the spinous processes of the withers bending toward that side. This harder side to "rock" is often referred as the "sticky side." Let your fingers' four T's give you direct feedback on the evenness of the transverse processes' alignments and on the quality of the muscle and fascia tissue attaching to these early thoracic vertebrae. To assist your evaluation, consider checking the alignment of the spinous processes that form the withers from above by standing on a block, as shown in figure 17.4.

Gently palpate the withers with one hand and try to locate which exact spinous process, or processes are out of line, between spinous process 7 to 11 as shown in figure 17.5.

*17.5 Palpating the Withers from Above*

Misaligned first thoracic vertebrae can be adjusted by a veterinarian chiropractor. However, for the purpose of your evaluation, it is important for you to figure out first if your horse's withers are misaligned and if so, whether the misalignment is simply an isolated problem or whether it is secondary, meaning compensatory, to another more serious problem coming from the back or feet, or both.

## POINT 7: THE REST OF THE THORACIC SPINE

A healthy thoracic spine is crucial for good riding. Any misalignment among the thoracic vertebrae will strongly affect the horse's performance in both straight and bending exercises. Furthermore, it could contribute to an inflammation of the back muscles, commonly known as a "cold back" condition. Checking the rest of the thoracic spine with your palpation skills will give you precise and precious information on the following:

The alignment of the rest of thoracic vertebrae (T12 to T18)

The relation between the last thoracic vertebrae (T18) and first lumbar vertebra (L1)

The presence of scoliosis, lordosis, kissing spines, or vertebral fusion

The amount of muscular tension attaching to the entire back

The tension in the local fascia layers

The level of inflammation in these structures, if any

Run your fingers along the rest of thoracic spine from the withers to the last rib. To do this you can use either of two approaches. One is done standing on the side of the horse, as shown in figure 17.6, doing one side at a time, and later comparing your feedback.

The other approach is done standing on a mounting block, as shown in figure 17.7. This elevated position will give you a better view and appreciation of the entire thoracic spine.

Standing on a mounting block with one hand on each side of the spine, run both hands at once from the withers to the sacrum. If you pick up any bump along this section of the spine, it indicates unevenness, possibly a sore location. You might determine if there is some degree of malformation such as scoliosis, a condition in which the spine is deviated laterally off the median plane. Depending on its severity, scoliosis can cause mild to severe strain on the ligaments and muscular support structures, and to some degree can limit the horse's ability to perform evenly on both sides.

Let your fingers' four T's give you direct feedback on the degree of unevenness of the thoracic transverse processes' alignments and on the quality of the muscle and fascia tissue attaching to that particular location. Verify the elasticity component of these muscle and fascia tissue throughout the back. Any hardening of the fibers indicates the presence of extra compensatory tension.

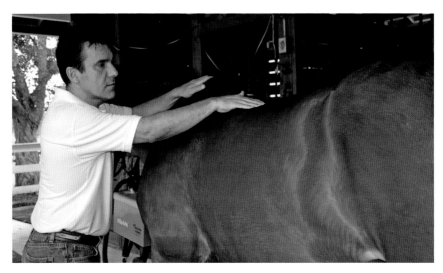

*17.6 Checking the Thoracic Spine, Standing at the Side of the Horse*

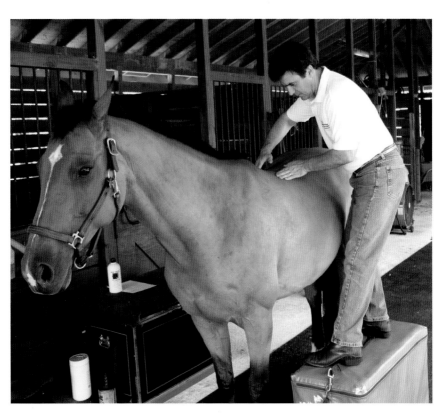

*17.7 Checking the Thoracic Spine, Standing on a Block*

A misaligned thoracic vertebra can easily be adjusted by a veterinarian chiropractor. However, for the purpose of your massage palpation evaluation, it is important for you to figure out if there is a thoracic misalignment, and if there is, whether it is an isolated problem or if it is secondary, meaning compensatory, to another more serious problem such as a sore forelimb, a sore hip or sacrum, or possibly a saddle or a rider problem.

## POINT 8: THE RIB CAGE

A well-developed rib cage is a good feature to have on a horse because it shows a good lung capacity. However, any soreness between the ribs (possibly from a kick or blow) or any rib displacement would affect and possibly limit the horse's ability to bend to the same side. Checking the rib cage with your palpation skills will give you precise and precious information on the following:

The alignment of the ribs on either side of the thorax

The amount of muscular tension between the ribs

The amount of muscular tension on the last two floating ribs

The amount of muscular tension on the first rib

The amount of muscular tension attaching to the sternum, the front part of the rib cage

The tension in the local fascia layers

The level of inflammation in these structures, if any

First, run both your hands smoothly and in full contact with the rib cage, from the scapula to the last two ribs, as shown in figure 17.8.

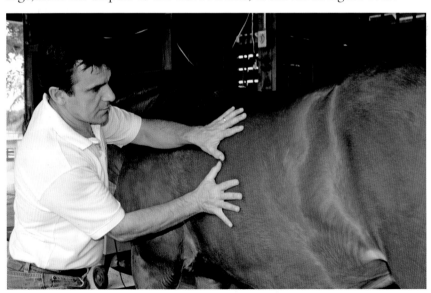

*17.8 Checking the Rib Cage, Standing at the Side of the Horse*

If a rib is out of alignment, you will feel it sticking out as you gently pass your hands over the horse. If no rib sticks out, good!

Next, standing on a block, run your fingers from the withers to the last rib, about 2 to 3 inches away from the spinous process of the thoracic spine, along the upper angle of the rib cage, as shown in figure 17.9. Do one side at a time and compare your feedback.

If you pick up any unevenness in the alignment of the ribs, it indicates a misaligned rib. Let your fingers' four T's give you direct feedback on the evenness of the ribs and on the quality of the muscle and fascia tissue attaching to these misaligned ribs by running your fingers in between them. This will help you determine the level of soreness and inflammation, if any.

If you had determined earlier some degree of scoliosis when checking the thoracic spine, you will find tension in the head of the ribs on both the contracted and the convex sides of that scoliosis.

*17.9 Checking the Rib Cage, Standing on a Block*

A rib sticking out can easily be adjusted by a veterinarian chiropractor. However, for the purpose of your massage palpation evaluation, it is important for you to figure out if this rib cage misalignment is an isolated problem, or if it is associated with a thoracic vertebra misalignment, secondary, meaning compensatory, to another more serious problem such as a sore sacrum, a misaligned withers, or a saddle or a rider problem.

## POINT 9: THE LUMBAR SPINE

The lumbar vertebrae are the biggest and strongest of all the vertebrae in the spine, besides the sacrum. This is due to the many strong muscle groups that attach onto them: the hip flexors and extensors, the back extensors, and the abdominals, just to name a few. When there is some discomfort (such as arthritis) or possible misalignment among the lumbar vertebrae, it will quickly reflect on the rest of the back structure. Depending on the severity, muscular and fascia compensation will also develop in both the fore and the hind limbs, affecting their performance. Checking the lumbar area of your horse will give you good information on the following:

The alignment of his lumbar vertebrae (L1 to L6)

The amount of muscular tension attaching to his lumbar vertebrae

The tension in the local fascia layers

The level of inflammation in these structures, if any

Run your fingers along the lumbar spine from L1 to the sacrum. You can do that by standing on the side of the horse, as shown in figure 17.10, doing one side at a time and comparing your feedback.

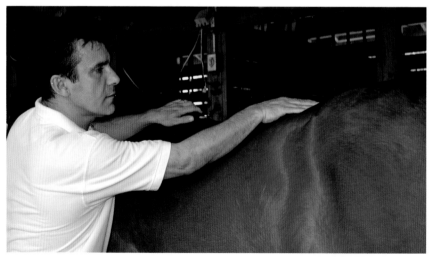

*17.10 Checking the Lumbar Spine, Standing at the Side of the Horse*

However, standing on a mounting block is preferable for a good evaluation of the lumbar area, because this allows you to stand directly above it. Run your hand along the lumbar section of the spine, all the way to the sacrum, as shown in figure 17.11.

If you pick up any unevenness in the alignment of this section of the spine, it indicates a sore location. Let your fingers' four T's give you direct feedback on the evenness of the lumbar transverse processes' alignments and on the quality of the muscle and fascia tissue attaching to these lumbar vertebrae. If you pick up some soreness by L6 and the sacrum, this could indicate a "sacralization," a condition in which the last lumbar vertebra fuses with the sacrum. This would affect the horse's overall performance. If you suspect this is the case, contact your veterinarian chiropractor.

A misaligned lumbar vertebra can easily be adjusted by a veterinarian chiropractor. However, for the purpose of your massage palpation evaluation, it is important for you to figure out if this lumbar misalignment is an isolated problem or if it is secondary, meaning compensatory, to another, more serious problem such as a sore sacrum, sore withers, a misfitting saddle, a limb or a shoeing problem, or possibly a previous rider.

*17.11 Checking the Lumbar Spine, Standing on a Block*

# POINT 10: THE SACRUM

The sacrum is made of five fused sacral vertebrae. It provides very strong anchoring for the gluteal and the hamstring muscle groups, the biggest muscles responsible for the power generated for the retraction of the hind limbs. The sacrum is embedded in the dorsal and the ventral sacroiliac ligaments. These ligaments provide reinforcement to the sacroiliac articulations and allow some "floating" between the caudal end of the sacrum and the iliac crest of the pelvis.

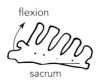
flexion

sacrum

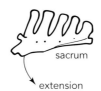
sacrum

extension

*17.12 The Sacrum*

Due to its physical location, a sacrum can be "out" in several ways:

It can be in flexion, where its cranial portion sticks up.

It can be in extension, where its cranial part sinks in.

It can be "sticky" on one of its articular edges.

Any misalignment in the sacrum area would directly affect the hind limbs' performance and cause serious compensation factors to develop over the back and forelegs. Checking the sacrum and tail will give you needed information on the following:

The alignment of the sacrum in relation to the pelvis (sacroiliac joint)

The amount of muscular tension attaching to the sacrum

The tension in the local fascia layers

The level of inflammation in these structures, if any

Proportional to its displacement, a misaligned sacrum is usually a painful condition for the horse, so use very light pressure when first starting to palpate its edges. Let your fingers' four T's give you direct feedback on the state of the tissues over and adjacent to the sacrum.

You can palpate the sacrum by standing on the side of the horse, as shown in figure 17.13.

Using your fingertips as probes, gently friction the edge of the sacrum, checking one side at a time and then comparing the feedback for each side later. If the horse reacts to your touch by crouching, it is a sign of soreness, possibly inflammation. This can be due to some muscle soreness if your animal is in heavy training, or to some misalignment in the sacroiliac joint. If you suspect inflammation is the case, contact your veterinarian for proper diagnosis and a course of treatment.

*17.13 Checking the Sacrum, Standing at the Side of the Horse*

Standing on a mounting block is a better way to palpate all aspects of the sacrum at once, as shown in figure 17.14.

From this position, looking down on the horse, palpate the edges of the sacrum by simply pressing your fingertips firmly on one side first, then on the other. If the sacrum is healthy, the horse should not have any reaction to your pressure. If one edge is tight, or "sticky," the horse will flinch a little under your pressure. This is a sign telling you that side needs work. Usually the gluteal and hamstring muscles attaching to that side of the sacrum show strong tension and possibly some inflammation, often seen during training.

If the sacroiliac joint is subluxated (mildly dislocated) there will be an obvious inflammation resulting from the instability of the joint on that side. Also you will feel strong tension in the gluteal and hamstring muscles attaching to that area. The excess muscle tension is a response from the muscle groups to stabilize the sacroiliac joint.

Next, proceed to palpate the cranial portion of the sacrum. If the anterior aspect of the sacrum appears to stick out abnormally, this reveals that the sacrum is in flexion. If this resulted from the mechanics of the hip and limb, the horse's hooves would be externally rotated. If the cranial portion of the sacrum appears to sink in abnormally, this reveals that the sacrum is in extension. If that happens to be the case, the horse's hooves would be internally rotated, as shown in figure 17.15.

*17.14 Checking the Sacrum, Standing on a Block*

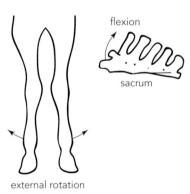

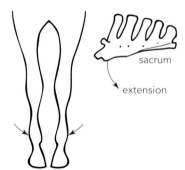

*17.15 Sacrum, with Hooves*

Whichever way you decide to evaluate the sacrum of your horse, always be gentle. If you pick up signs of inflammation such as soreness to touch, heat, and possible swelling, it is a sure sign that the sacrum is misaligned in some way. In that case, contact your veterinarian chiropractor for a better diagnosis and course of treatment.

When no signs of inflammation are present, it's a good sign that the sacrum is in good working position. However, keep in mind that sometimes the "sticky" side of a sacrum might not show signs of inflammation and yet might somehow affect the horse's gait on that side to some extent. When you're not sure, contact your veterinarian.

## POINT 11: THE TAIL

The horse uses his tail as a balancer during movement. As the prolongation of the sacrum, the tail can reveal sacroiliac problems. When trotting, the horse's tail should remain straight. If it is held clamped to one side, it usually indicates a misaligned sacrum on the same side. Checking the tail will give you precious information on the following:

The alignment of the coccygeal vertebrae in relation to the sacrum

The amount of muscular tension in the tail muscles

The level of inflammation in these structures, if any

Use some gentle strokings along the sacrum bone and down the buttocks before picking up the tail. Leave your left hand on the sacrum. Use your right hand to take hold of the tail a few inches from its base, as shown in figure 17.16.

*17.16 Picking up the Tail*

Bring the tail up and gently move it in a circle two or three times starting clockwise, and then counterclockwise two or three times, as shown in figure 17.17.

During these movements, take note of any resistance or restriction found in moving the tail to either side. If one side appears much harder to rotate than the other, it is a sign of unbalanced muscle tension often seen with the case of a "sticky" sacrum on the same side.

Next, still holding the tail gently, position yourself at the back of the horse and start to pull the tail progressively toward you, as shown in figure 17.18.

Use only 1 to 2 pounds of pressure maximum. This is not a contest to see how hard you can pull. Use your common sense. Never pull to the point of discomfort. As you hold the stretch, usually you will feel the horse pulling slightly forward and lowering his head. It is his way to adjust the stretch to his liking. Maintain the stretch for approximately one minute, or the equivalent of eight deep breaths, unless the horse shows discomfort. During that time the horse, feeling good, will respond positively by chewing and further lowering his head.

Past the minute, maintain the stretch with one hand, while softly squeezing each vertebra between the thumb and fingers of your other hand, from the base of the tail down, as shown in figure 17.19.

Make note of the tail's flexibility, looking for sore spots and possible inflammation. The tail usually consists of eighteen coccygeal vertebrae, although this number can vary considerably among breeds. Be gentle during your evaluation of the tail.

*17.17 Tail Rotation*

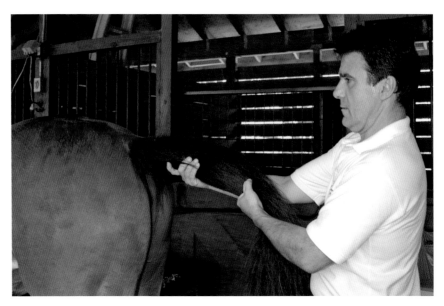

*17.18 Tail Stretch*

*17.19 Tail Stretch with Squeezings*

When ready to release the stretch, please proceed progressively. To abruptly let go can be painful to the horse. When done, stroke the hindquarters and sacrum area for a few seconds. This will make the horse feel good, and completes the tail evaluation.

*Warning:* If when you start stretching the tail feels "loose" at its attachment site (with half an inch give before the actual stretch starts), stop at once. You could be hurting the horse. The looseness means the horse has a not-uncommon joint problem. If you continue to pull the tail, you could produce a strain. If this is the case, skip the stretching. Have your veterinarian check this condition.

# POINT 12: THE HIP

The pelvis is made of the ilium, ischium, and pubis bones. The bony landmark known as the point of hip is the tuber coxae portion of the iliac crest.

For the hipbones, you are looking for any misalignment that would affect the hind limbs performance.

Checking the pelvis will give you good information on the following:

The positioning of the pelvis in relation to the spine

The amount of muscular tension attaching to the pelvis

The tension in the local fascia layers

The level of inflammation in these structures, if any

## PELVIS MISALIGNMENT

Looking from behind at your horse standing square, you might see the rump higher on one side. This can be due either to a pelvic rotation or an iliac bone up-slip and a down-slip on the other side of the hip. In such case, a horse usually has a hard time standing square or maintaining his gaits during exercise. Proceed to a palpation, standing from behind the horse with both hands over the points of hip and feel for which one is depressed and which one is elevated. Also palpate the various muscle groups (glutes, hamstrings, quads) on both sides to detect which muscles are tighter. If your horse presents some pelvis misalignment, and depending on how long since the horse had that pelvis rotated, you might find muscular and myofascial restrictions in the pelvis and gluteal fasciae, possibly reaching to the thoracolumbar and abdominal fasciae as well as the fascia latae.

## PELVIS TILT

If the horse naturally stands camped out, he could be subject to an *anterior pelvic tilt*. This is most commonly seen with jumpers, due to the weight of the rider landing on the horse's back while his legs are still extended back after clearing high obstacles. The anterior pelvic tilt creates a fair amount of tension in the gluteal and hamstring muscles groups, as well as the gluteal, femoral, crural, and possibly over the fascia latae.

If the horse naturally stands camped under, he could be subject to a *posterior pelvic tilt*. This is a less common condition usually secondary to a backward fall. The posterior pelvic tilt creates a fair amount of tension in the back and abdominal muscles groups as well as the thoracolumbar, femoral, and possibly over the gluteal fasciae.

## UNILATERAL AND BILATERAL HIP MISALIGNMENT

A unilateral hip misalignment condition is characterized by a displacement of the ilium bone laterally and the ischium bone of the same side medially. The hip on the other side has not moved. This not uncommon condition often happens when a horse runs through a narrow space and catches his hip on a structure. At rest, the horse stands with the leg slightly behind and turned outward.

Sometimes when the horse catches a hip, the impact is so great that the entire hip shifts. The bilateral hip misalignment signs and symptoms are basically the same as with the unilateral iliac misalignment, except that the opposite side is now showing its ilium being displaced forward and its ischium being displaced laterally.

To check your horse's hip alignment, place yourself behind the horse and move the tail up and to the side, as shown in figure 17.20.

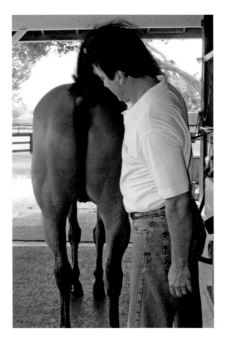

*17.20 Lifting the Tail to See Median Line*

On a healthy horse, you can see the median line going straight in between the two thighs. If the hip has shifted, you will see the ischium of the affected side being closer to the median line, and when reaching the point of hip with your hands, you will note the ilium of the same affected side sticking out laterally.

## STRESS POINTS

Following the palpation of the skeletal features of the back, proceed to supervise the following muscle locations for potential stress points. (See chapter 5, pages 59–61, for the stress point location chart for better visualization.) Use gentle kneading massage movements to work the following muscles and effleurage massage movement to flow from one point to the other:

SP20 is found in front of the withers, by the origin tendon of the *longissimus dorsi muscle* located in the deep muscle layer, as shown in figure 17.21.

SP21 is found close to the last rib, by the insertion tendon of the *iliocostalis dorsi muscle* located in the deep muscle layer, as shown in figure 17.22.

SP22 is found along the edge of the hipbone, by the origin tendon of *the external abdominal oblique muscle* located in the superficial muscle layer, as shown in figure 17.23.

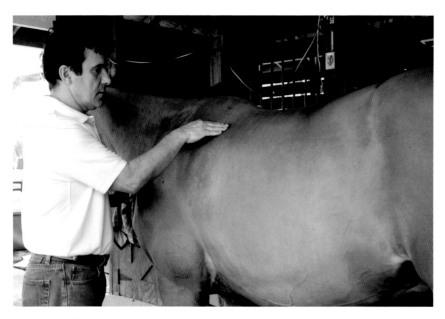

*17.21* **Checking SP20**

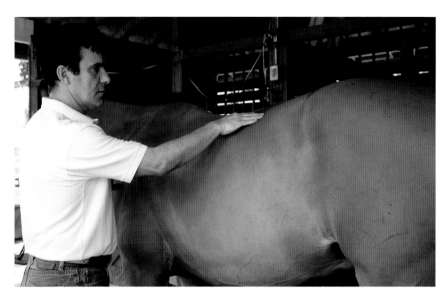

*17.22 Checking SP21*

SP23 is found on the sternum by the tenth rib, right by the insertion tendon of the *external abdominal oblique muscle* located in the superficial muscle layer, as shown in figure 17.24.

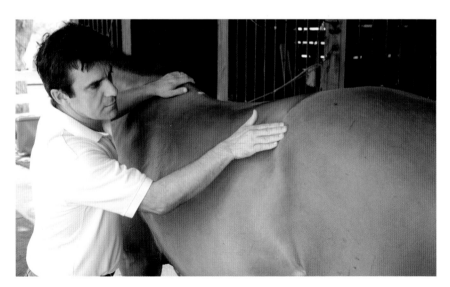

*17.23 Checking SP22*

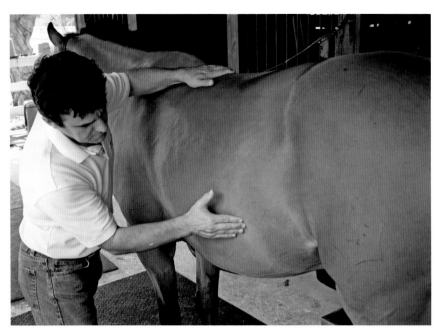

*17.24 Checking SP23*

SP24 is found in front of the point of hip, by the origin tendon of the *internal abdominal oblique muscles* located in the deep muscle layer, as shown in figure 17.25.

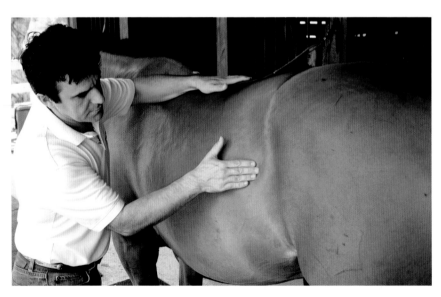

*17.25 Checking SP24*

SP25 is found in front of the point of the hip, by the origin tendon of the *transverse abdominal muscle* located in the deep muscle layer, as shown in figure 17.26.

SP26 is found between the tenth and eleventh ribs, in the *intercostal muscle* located in the deep muscle layer, as shown in figure 17.27.

Having a thorough knowledge of all the stress points found in the body of the horse will contribute tremendously to your evaluation.

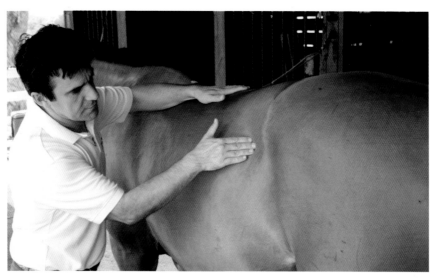

*17.26 Checking SP25*

*17.27 Checking SP26*

## STRETCHING THE BACK

Stretching the back and tail of your horse will further contribute to your evaluation of your horse. Please review figures 4.11 through 4.15 in chapter 4 for details on the various back and tail stretches you can perform with your animal.

If your horse appears restricted in performing his back stretch, it can simply indicate some muscle tension in his back, limiting the benefit of the stretch. It can also reveal that the horse's back vertebrae are not properly aligned, and the stretch is causing some pinching and discomfort, resulting in a limited stretch. In that case, it is important to contact a veterinarian chiropractor to adjust the back.

# 18

## THE FORELIMB: POINTS 13 TO 19

The forelimb apparatus acts as a steering mechanism and as a shock absorber to comfortably stabilize the thorax at all gaits and during the landing phase of a jump. The forelimb is made up of strong bones, ligaments, and muscles. Please take a moment to review figures 5.5, 5.8, 5.9, 5.12, 5.13, and 5.15 in chapter 5 to refresh your memory on the actual location of these bones, ligaments and muscles.

Conducting a massage palpation evaluation of points 13 to 19 over the forelimbs will help you determine some very important components of the horse's health and performance:

The shoulder blades, since they are very important for good performance.

The health of all the other leg joints (point of shoulders, elbows, knees, fetlocks, and pastern joints) and associated ligaments: Healthy joints in the forelegs are important to good motion.

The potential stress points present in the foreleg musculature: This information will help you better understand where your horse carries his stress and why.

Keep in mind that the extra weight of the rider and saddle directly and constantly affects this very structure in the horse at work. Good flexibility of the foreleg is vital to good performance. A horse uses his foreleg to direct and balance the rest of his body. Usually a nodding movement of the horse's head—the head rising when the foot of the lame leg is on the ground and falling with the sound one—is an indication of some sort of front leg lameness. If any discomfort, and eventually any lameness, arises in either of the forelimbs, it will quickly affect the rest of the body. Your massage palpation evaluation will allow you to identify areas of soreness and possibly inflammation along the various parts of the foreleg.

# LEG CONFORMATION

Good conformation of the forehand is important. When standing in front of the horse and regarding the foreleg as a whole, an ideal structure can be identified by a theoretical perpendicular plumb line that travels downward from a point at the center of the scapulohumeral joint (shoulder joint), dividing the limb equally through the elbow, knee, and fetlock, and ending at a point on the center of the hoof, as shown in figure 18.1.

When standing at the side the horse, an ideal conformation structure can be identified by a theoretical plumb line that should travel downward from the tuber spinae on the spine of the scapula, dividing the limb equally, through the fetlock and ending just behind the heel, as shown in figure 18.2.

Please review all the conformation details in chapter 6, page 62. Understanding these guidelines will help you to quickly evaluate what your horse is showing you and where you will find his musculoskeletal stress.

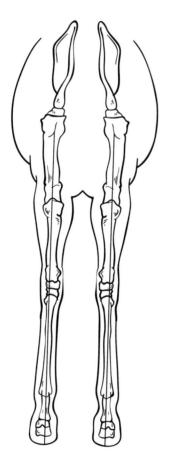

*18.1 Front Leg Ideal Cranial Plumb Line*

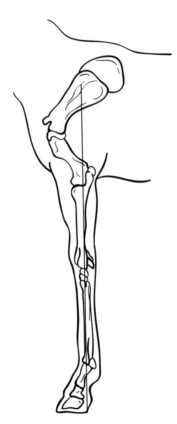

*18.2 Front Lateral Plumb Line*

The added weight on the horse's back (tack, saddle, and rider) transfers onto the forelegs and can cause of a lot of problems, not to mention possible structural deformities such as being over at the knee or having bowed legs. The opinion on the type and suitability of the shoulder angles may vary with different individuals depending on the discipline contemplated.

As you start on one side, let your fingers' four T's give you direct feedback on the tonicity of the muscles and fascia tissues attaching over that area. When done, repeat the same procedure on the other side. Then compare your feedback sensations. Evaluate these muscles and the local fascia tissues. Look for potential trigger points or possible stress points. If your future plans include doing a fair amount of jumping and/or lateral work with that particular horse, those muscles need to be in good physical condition.

As mentioned earlier, if you are performing the PEP on a young horse, he might not be comfortable with you grabbing his foreleg. Be patient, smile, and praise the horse with your soft voice to build up his confidence. Make him feel safe. Within a few minutes he will relax and agree with your demand. The same might happen when you start stretching his foreleg, but no worries; maintain your calmness and your horse will comply. He might resist a little at the very beginning because of his strong character, but he will soon realize that you are not a threat and will comply with your request. If you are relaxed, the horse will relax.

## POINT 13: THE SHOULDER BLADE

The shoulder blade is also known as the scapula. Ample length of the scapula is essential to provide enough room for all the powerful shoulder muscles to anchor. Also, the scapular angle will determine the horse's stride. The more upright the shoulder, the shorter the stride. The straightness of the leg unfortunately can result in an undue concussion on the entire foreleg. This is not so desirable for a jumper, but very desirable for a trotter or pacer at the track. The more angles to the shoulder, the longer the stride and the more "spring" benefit to the leg, especially when jumping. Full action of the shoulder will happen if there is enough length of back to accommodate the shoulder's obliqueness. Checking the shoulder with your palpation skills will give you precise information on the following:

The quality of the shoulder girdle muscles attaching onto the scapula

The quality of the scapular muscles attaching onto the humerus

The tension in the local fascia layers

The level of inflammation in these structures, if any

## THE SHOULDER GIRDLE MUSCLES

The shoulder girdle muscles anchor on the scapula and attach the fore-limb onto the axial skeleton. Position yourself on the side of the horse and use the SEW approach (see chapter 2, page 17) to warm up the entire shoulder blade area, as shown in figure 18.3.

Then, adjust your posture to face the shoulder and palpate the trapez-ius and rhomboideus, as shown in figure 18.4.

Both these muscles should feel strong, but not too tight. Excessive tightness in these two muscles indicates possible problems in the leg, since the horse would tense these two muscles to pull the leg up in order to avoid adding weight on it. Poor saddle fitting could be another rea-son for strong abnormal tension in these two muscles.

Then check the serratus ventralis, with both its cervicis and thoracis portions, as shown in figure 18.5. Use your left hand over the serratus ventralis cervicis and your right hand over the serratus ventralis thoracis.

These two portions sustain a lot of stress when the horse has to jump extremely high fences. Sometimes, if the horse appears sore upon your palpation of the serratus ventralis cervicis only, it could indicate discom-fort in the lower cervical area, in the first rib, or both.

The subscapularis muscle, located between the scapula and the rib cage, is not readily palpable. However, you can stretch it by gently bring-ing the leg laterally, as shown in figure 18.6.

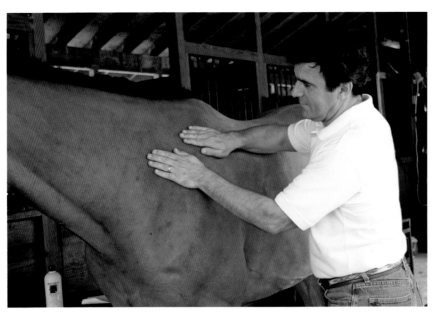

*18.3 Standing by Horse, Warming Up the Shoulder Blade*

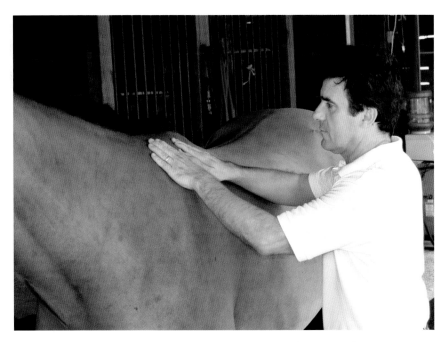

*18.4 Standing by Horse, Checking the Trapezius and Rhomboideus*

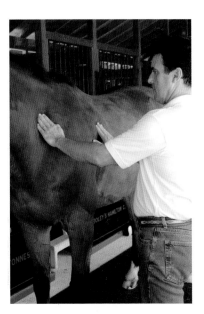

*18.5 Standing by Horse,
Checking the Serratus
Ventralis Cervicis and
Thoracis*

*18.6 Stretching the Foreleg
Laterally to Affect the
Subscapularis Muscle*

As you gently and progressively stretch the leg laterally, the horse will let go and loosen his shoulder muscles. If the horse resists your stretch, it is a sign of tension. Because this particular stretch is very unusual to the horse, consider repeating it several times. As your horse feels more comfortable with it, he will relax more and more.

## THE SCAPULAR MUSCLES

Use a gentle double-hand friction approach to palpate the supraspinatus, the infraspinatus, the teres minor and teres major, and the deltoideus, as shown in figure 18.7. Let your fingers' four T's (see chapter 1, page 3) give you direct feedback on the tonicity of these muscles and local fascia tissue.

If the supraspinatus and infraspinatus muscles appear sore and somehow atrophied, this could indicate a "Sweeny" condition resulting from a partial damage to the suprascapular nerve. Usually a horse with a chronic Sweeny condition is said to "pop" his shoulder when walking; this "popping" corresponds to a quick shoulder abduction when the horse bears weight on the affected limb. It would have been noticeable during your REP.

If, from your riding evaluation program (REP), you felt the horse had some restricted foreleg motion with one of his forelimbs, this could mean that he had previously strained some of his shoulder muscles, most likely the serratus ventralis, both the cervical and thoracic portions. If you are planning to use this horse for jumping, ensure that he is fully recovered.

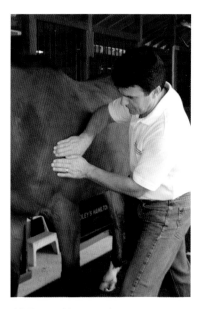

*18.7 Double-Hand Friction over the Suprascapular Muscles*

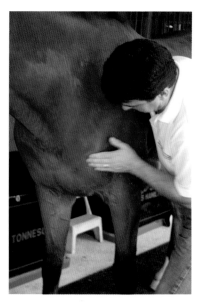

*18.8 Gentle Friction over the Biceps Brachii*

Such deep muscle strain can be hard to heal. Also, check the alignment of the withers because any discomfort in that particular area would affect the brachial nervous plexus governing the shoulder structures.

## POINT 14: THE POINT OF SHOULDER

Checking the point of shoulder with your palpation skills will give you information on the following:

The quality of the muscles attaching onto the lower scapula and the head of humerus
The bicipital bursa
The tension in the local fascia layers
The level of inflammation in these structures, if any

Use a light touch when approaching the point of shoulder, since it might be slightly sore to the horse.

Use gentle friction over the front of the scapulohumeral joint. Work the biceps brachii and the bicipital bursa, as shown in figure 18.8. The bursa, which protects the tendon of the biceps brachii, is located underneath the biceps brachii tendon in the bicipital groove of the cranial prominence of the lateral tuberosity of the humerus. The humerus should be well developed to provide solid anchoring to the powerful shoulder and arm muscles.

Soreness of the biceps brachii muscle and possibly of the bicipital bursa can be the result of overuse, or of a direct trauma such as when a horse hits a fence or receives a kick from another horse. This area can get seriously traumatized and become inflamed. The result of such inflammation is a reduced mobility in the point shoulder and a shorter stride of the afflicted leg.

If, after you proceed to your PEP over both shoulders, you feel that one side is somehow "slimmer," it could reveal that the horse has had suffered some shoulder trauma, resulting in some degree of scapulohumeral joint instability. If so, be thorough in your PEP. Also, if you perceive some degree of inflammation in this area, contact your veterinarian for a proper diagnosis.

## POINT 15: THE ELBOW

Checking the elbow with your palpation skills will give you important information on the following:

The quality of the triceps muscle attaching onto the point of elbow
The tension in the local fascia layers
The level of inflammation in these structures, if any

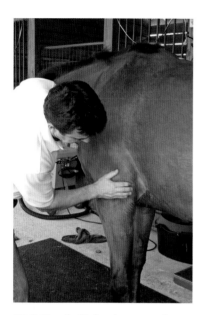

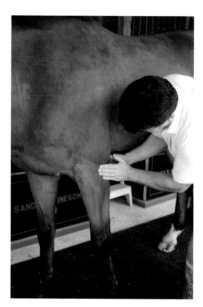

*18.9 Gentle Palpation over the
    Point of Elbow*

*18.10 Gentle Palpation of the
    Upper Radius Bone*

Palpation of the elbow will reveal the condition of this important joint. Position yourself on the side of the horse to palpate the elbow, as shown in figure 18.9.

The elbow should be clearly defined, standing clear from the ribs. Any swelling over the elbow could be revealing of a chronic inflammation known as "capped elbow," maybe from an old fracture of the point of elbow or from arthritis. A horse with arthritis in his elbow will be nodding as the afflicted leg touches the ground during a trotting exercise. Not much can be done for this condition, whether it is a closed arthritis from natural wear and tear, or an open arthritis from a kick or wound.

The elbow joint should stand clear of the body. If the elbow turns in it will cause the feet to be turned out, and in the opposite, the feet will be turned in. Neither case is desirable since they cause undue strain on the fetlock and feet, not to mention interferences when brushing and speedy-cutting.

Let your fingers' four T's give you direct feedback on the tonicity of the muscle and fascia tissues attaching over that area.

If you feel the horse reacts to your palpation of the extensor muscles of the elbow (triceps brachii) and the forearm (extensor carpi radialis), or if you feel that the triceps and the foreleg extensor muscles appear somehow atrophied, it can indicate some form of trauma to the radial nerve (a kick or another form of trauma). A lower neck (C7–T1) misalignment, especially with the head of the first rib displacement, can also be the root of this discomfort to the radial nerve. Weak forearms that show lack of muscle tone and tendon weakness will predispose the horse to a greater risk of strain.

The radius bone of the forearm should be long, thick, and well developed. Consider palpating the upper aspect of the radius bone, just below the elbow, as shown in figure 18.10.

This move will help you determine the presence of excess scar tissue possibly from an old injury such as a partial fracture.

As you palpate the lower aspect of the radius, do not forget to palpate the area of the superior check ligament on the lateral aspect of the posterior radius bone, above the accessory carpal bone, as shown in figure 18.11.

## POINT 16: THE KNEE JOINT

Checking the knee with your palpation skills will give you good information on the following:

The quality of the flexor and extensor muscle tendons going by the knee

The quality of the knee aponeurosis

The tension in the local fascia layers

The level of inflammation in these structures, if any

Palpation of the knee will reveal the condition of this important joint. Position yourself on the side of the horse to palpate the knee joint, as shown in figure 18.12.

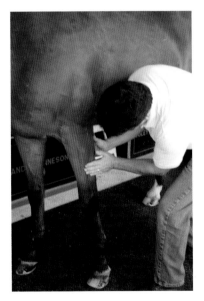

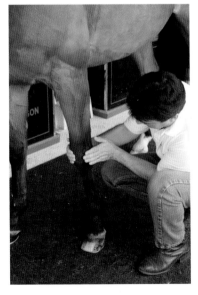

*18.11 Gentle Palpation of the Lower Radius Bone*

*18.12 Standing by Horse, Palpation of the Knee*

The knee should be broad and flat, showing a clean outline with no bony lumps. If the knee is swollen and hard, it could indicate a chronic inflammation resulting from an old injury such as a fracture of one of the carpal bones, some bone spurs from arthritis, or capsulitis. Palpate the knee thoroughly. Consider some gentle frictions over the front of the knee to check the extensor retinaculum, and over the back of the knee to check the flexor retinaculum, as shown in figure 18.13.

Any undue soreness could indicate some form of arthritis. If the outline of the joint is bumpy, it is called "open arthritis" and is the result of some sort of trauma. If the outline is not bumpy but hot, it is called "enclosed arthritis" and is the result of regular wear and tear. A horse with arthritis in his knee will be nodding as the afflicted leg touches the ground during a trotting exercise.

A horse with narrow and imperfectly formed knees, especially with short forearms and upright shoulders, is predisposed to carpitis, an inflammation of the knee joint. This overall conformation favors an exaggerated movement of the knee joint leading to early wear and tear (enclosed arthritis). Carpitis is often seen in thoroughbreds and jumpers. As much as a young horse with carpitis responds well to massage, hot fomentations, and strong liniments, this is not a good predisposition for being a jumper. Let your fingers' four T's give you direct feedback on the tonicity of the muscle and fascia tissues attaching over that area.

Conformation faults such as "calf-kneed," also known as "back at the knee," make the horse more prone to tendon strain and severe problems in the joint itself. The opposite condition, "buck-kneed," also known as "knee-sprung," is not as tough on the horse, but will cause tenderness at the joint and is considered a serious conformation fault.

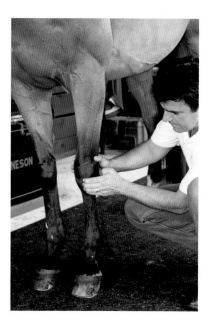

*18.13 **Gentle Friction of the Knee***

# POINT 17: THE CANON BONE, THE SUSPENSORY LIGAMENT, AND THE FLEXOR TENDON

Checking the canon bone, the suspensory ligament, and the flexor tendon with your palpation skills will give you information about the following:

The quality of the canon bone

The quality of the flexor tendon

The quality of the suspensory ligament

The tension in the local fascia layers

The level of inflammation in these structures, if any

The canon bone should be reasonably short and strong with clearly defined tendon behind them. A long canon bone can be stressful over the flexor tendon and suspensory ligaments. Palpation of the canon will reveal the condition of several important structures. Position yourself on the side of the horse to palpate the canon bone, as shown in figure 18.14.

Any thickening in the upper third of the canon bone would indicate an older injury either to the bone itself (green splints or fracture) or to the lower check ligament or the suspensory ligament. Any swelling behind the upper third of the canon, and possibly the knee, would indicate a possible chronic problem with the origin of the suspensory ligament or of the flexor tendon.

Any thickening over the middle of the canon bone indicates bucked shins or an old transverse fracture of the canon bone (from a kick or fall).

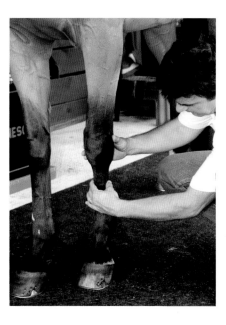

*18.14 **Standing by Horse, Palpation of the Canon Bone***

Any enlargement over the posterior aspect of the middle of the canon bone indicates an old injury, possibly chronic inflammation of a sprained tendon (bowed tendon) or ligament.

Any thickening over the lower third of the canon bone indicates epiphysis. Any inflammation in that area could reveal a sprained tendon or ligament, eventually wind puffs.

If you come to realize that the canon bone is narrower below the knee than above the fetlock joint, there is a risk of weakness in the bone and the tendons. This is known as "tied in below the knee."

To palpate the flexor tendons and the suspensory ligament, position yourself on the side of the horse and ask him for his leg. Bending his knee will relax the lower leg and make it easier for your work, as shown in figure 18.15.

Use your thumb and index finger to grab and gently twist the flexor tendons all along its course. You can also use some gentle thumb or finger frictions to evaluate the deeper suspensory ligament. Let your fingers' four T's give you direct feedback on the tonicity of the muscle tendon, ligament, and fascia tissues attaching over that area. On a healthy horse, both limbs should feel the same. If you detect a difference in heat between the two forelimbs, it indicates an undergoing condition.

If you feel a pronounced inflammation—swelling, heat, and soreness to touch—of the flexor tendon at the level of the knee, it can be related to a case of carpal tunnel syndrome, a condition seen more often in jumpers. Below the knee, on either side of the canon bone, check for splints, the ossification of the interosseus ligament resulting in a bony

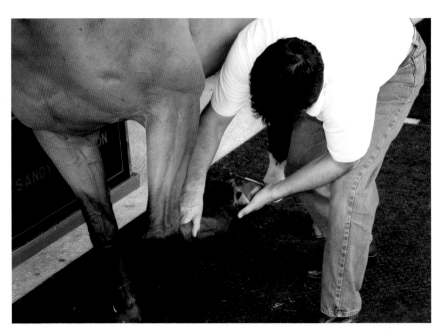

*18.15 **Knee Bent, Palpation of the Flexor Tendon and Suspensory Ligament***

enlargement that arises between the canon bone and the small metacarpal bones (second and fourth metacarpals). Old splints are not painful, but the most recent cases are painful on pressure. To check for a splint, run your thumb along the groove between the large and small bones on either side.

If you detect some swelling in mid-shaft, it can indicate an injury to the superficial and deep flexor tendons. Because of the mechanics of locomotion, this is the area where most strains occur, due to the excessive amount of stress put on them during the stride, the landing of a jump, quick turns, or other stressful maneuvers. Conformation and shoeing will also be a factor in the stress seen on these tendons.

Mid-shaft is also where the inferior check ligament blends with the deep digital flexor tendon on the medial aspect of the posterior canon bone. Injury to the inferior check ligament is common in standardbred trotters and pacers, and with horses shod with a long toe and low heel. Also, an unbalanced hoof with greater weight bearing upon the medial surface would stress the inferior check ligament. A horse with a sore inferior check ligament will have a hard time with a forward stretch of his affected foreleg.

You can palpate the origin of the suspensory ligament on the posterior surface of the lowest row of carpal bones and the upper aspect of the canon bone (third metacarpal). Other good locations to check the suspensory ligament are its attachment over the sesamoid bones, and its distal attachment by the extensor tendon in front of the hoof. If you suspect soreness in the suspensory ligament, use the following stretch to test it. Bring the horse's foreleg forward with the knee bent, supporting his forearm and holding his canon bone with your right arm, as shown in figure 18.16, and holding his hoof firmly with your left hand.

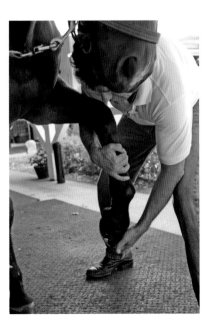

*18.16 Suspensory Ligament Stretch, Preparation*

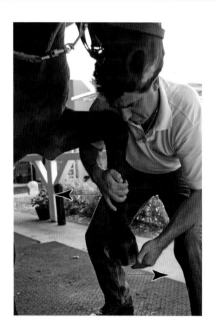

*18.17 Suspensory Ligament Stretch, Development*

Simultaneously, grab the canon at mid-shaft with the supporting arm's hand and pull back while with your other hand extends the hoof forward, as shown in figure 18.17.

If the suspensory ligament is healthy, the horse will not mind this stretch. If the horse reacts by retracting his leg, suspect desmitis, an inflammation of the supensory ligament.

During your palpation, a reaction along with any swelling, heat, and soreness should be perceived as a warning sign and you should contact your veterinarian immediately.

## POINT 18: THE FETLOCK

Checking the fetlock with your palpation skills will give you precise and precious information on the following:

The quality of the joint structure

The positioning of the sesamoid bones

The tension in the local fascia layers

The level of inflammation in these structures, if any

Palpation of the fetlock will reveal the condition of this joint. The fetlock should have a clean outline with no bumps or swelling. Position yourself on the side of the horse to palpate the fetlock joint, as shown in figure 18.18.

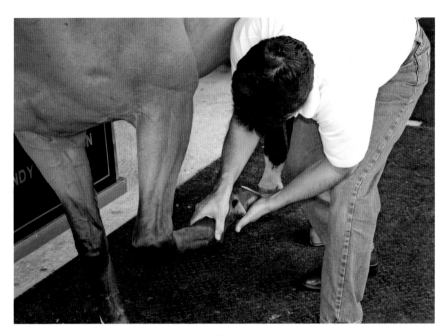

*18.18 Standing by Horse, Palpation of the Fetlock Joint*

Use some gentle frictions with your thumbs to check the entire fet-lock joint. Any tenderness reaction to touch over the fetlock may indi-cate an inflammation of the suspensory ligament, the deep flexor tendon, the sesamoid bones, or the navicular bone. Let your fingers' four T's give you direct feedback on the various structures of that area.

Any swelling in front of the fetlock joint can indicate a chronic prob-lem with the suspensory ligament, or possibly the joint capsule itself as in windgall, a sign of wear.

Excessive scar tissue over the medial aspect of the fetlock can indicate brushing from interference.

Any thickening on the posterior aspect of the fetlock joint, over the collateral and oblique sesamoidean ligaments, and the palmar annular lig-ament would indicate an older injury to either the sesamoid bones (frac-ture) or to the flexor tendon. Soreness of the sesamoid bones upon palpation can reveal a low-grade inflammation, which could lead to desmitis of the suspensory ligament if it flares up. Take the time to check the position of the sesamoid bones in relation to the hoof, as shown in figure 18.19.

Any discrepancy indicates contracted ligaments and fasciae in the lower leg that would affect the entire forelimb and ultimately the way the horse moves.

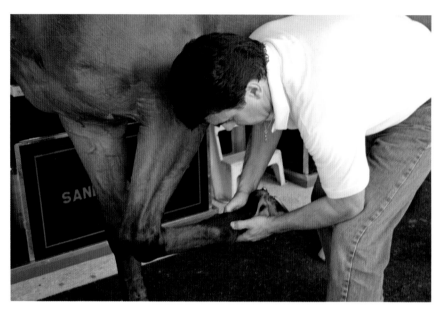

*18.19 Checking the Sesamoid Bones*

# POINT 19: THE PASTERN BONES AND HOOF

Checking pastern bones and the hoof with your palpation skills will reveal the condition of distal portion of the leg and will give you the following information:

The quality of the pastern joints

The quality of the hoof flexibility

The tension in the local fascia layers

The level of inflammation in these structures, if any

The pasterns should slope at an angle of 45 to 50 degrees, the same as the shoulder blade angle. The length of the pastern bones will vary with the breed. However, a pastern should be proportional to the rest of the leg without being too long, resulting in strain on ligaments and tendons, or too short, causing much concussion and associated problems. Position yourself on the side of the horse to palpate the fetlock joint, as shown in figure 18.20.

Hold the fetlock with one hand and palpate the pastern bones with the other. Any thickening in the first, second, or third pastern and its navicular bone would indicate an older injury to either the bone itself (fracture) or the flexor tendon or the suspensory ligament. Any swelling behind the pastern bones could be secondary to a chronic problem such as sesamoiditis, windgall, or possibly arthritis.

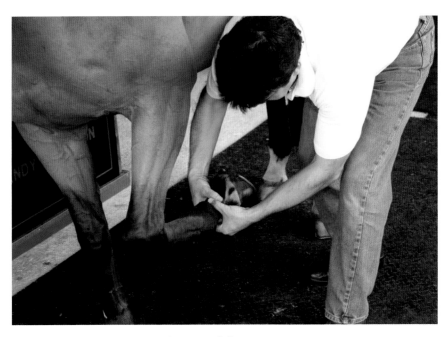

*18.20 Standing by Horse, Palpation of the Pastern Bones*

If you feel a bony enlargement on the pastern bones, suspect a ring-bone. This is due to arthritis because of repeated concussion, and often seen with jumpers. Do not friction too harshly over this ringbone, as it can be painful to touch.

Also, during your palpation and especially with jumper horses, pay attention to scar formation over the posterior aspect of the lower fore-leg as they might reveal "overreaching" wounds that are traumatic to the flexor apparatus, the fetlock joint, and possibly the pastern bones.

To evaluate the flexibility of the pastern bones, position your hands as shown in figure 18.21.

Hold the fist pastern bone (P1) firmly between your thumb and fingers of one hand, and with the other hand hold the front of the hoof. Gently rotate one way two to three times and then repeat going the other way. Observe and compare the quality of the motion from each side. You might feel the motion is very loose, which is good, or that it is restricted, which is a sign of tightness but not necessarily of unsound-ness. You might even feel and hear some crepitus, a dry, crackling sound as you proceed with the rotations. Repeat the same scenario, this time holding the second pastern bone (P2), as shown in figure 18.22

This exercise loosens the digital fascia, all the ligaments, and the joint capsules present in the lower aspect of the leg, and boosts circulation in that area. It is a good preventive exercise to practice on any horse regardless of age or discipline. As you practice this exercise on each of the four legs, you will get a good idea of the overall state of the lower legs of your horse.

*18.21 Checking the Pastern Bone (P1) Flexibility*

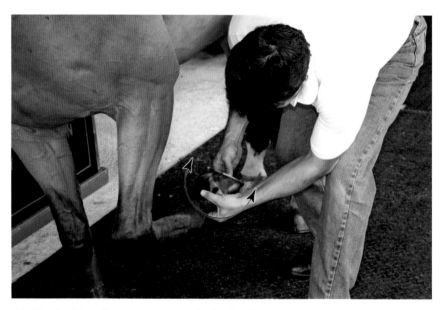

*18.22 Checking the Pastern Bone (P2) Flexibility*

# THE HOOF

Much can be said about hooves and how a horse should be shoed. In-depth information on this particular topic is beyond the scope of this book. However, briefly, hooves should face forward and be large, dense, and wide at the heels. If the heels appear contracted, suspect underlying problems. You should see a continuity in the slope of the hoof (45 to 50 degree) from the pasterns. If there is some inflammation on the coronet, suspect a quittor condition, an inflammation of the sinus of the foot that could lead to discharges and eventually an abscess.

It is hard to palpate the hoof. However, you can move it and stretch it to reveal the flexibility of the distal portion of the foreleg. While supporting the canon with the one hand, grab the hoof with the other hand and gently flex it, as shown in figure 18.23.

This will stretch the fascia cranially over the extensor muscle tendons. Sustain the flexion for a few seconds to reach its full potential. This approach will show you the level of flexibility in the flexion of that horse's foreleg. Compare later with the other foreleg.

Then reverse the process and extend the hoof. While supporting the canon with the one hand, grab the hoof with the other hand and gently extend it, as shown in figure 18.24.

This extension will stretch the same fascia tissue, but this time caudally over the flexor muscle tendons, the check ligament, the suspensory ligament, the palmar ligament, and the sesamoid ligaments. Hold the extension of the hoof for a few seconds to reach its full potential. This approach will show you the level of flexibility in the extension of that horse's foreleg. Compare later with the other foreleg.

Next, take a good look at the sole. The frog should be healthy looking. Do you see corns in the angles of the sole, the point between the wall of the hoof and the bars? This could indicate old bruises and possibly a condition known as pedal ostitis due to repeated concussions (in a jumper).

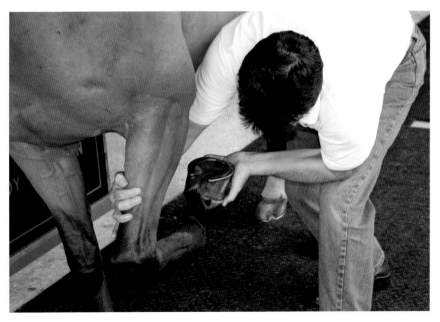

*18.23 Flexing the Hoof*

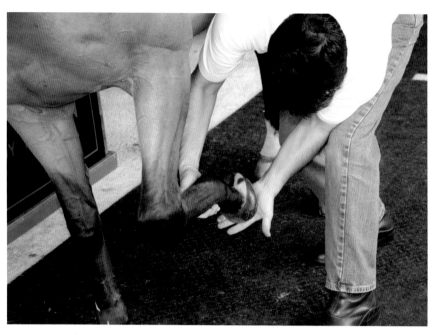

*18.24 Extending the Hoof*

Bad shoeing can lead to navicular disease. Check lateral cartilage as shown in figure 18.25.

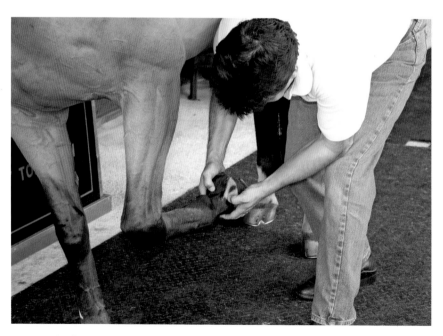

*18.25 Checking Lateral Cartilages of the Hoof*

If the cartilage is pliable and soft, it is a good sign. If one or both of them have hardened, this condition is known as sidebones. This may indicate inner stress due to shoeing, or compensation from another problem. Expansion of hoof by shoeing should be considered. Also look at the sole for traces of bruising, gravel, punctures, or cracks.

Finally, check on the hoof's degree of rotation around the pastern's axis. Hold the hoof as shown in figure 18.26.

Then gently but firmly rotate the hoof laterally, all the way to its limit. On a healthy horse, you should get a good 30 to 40 degrees away from the median line, as shown in figure 18.27.

Next, twist the hoof medially. You should get the same range of motion, as shown in figure 18.28.

A full range of motion is a sign of healthy ligaments and joints in the lower leg. If your horse does not have this full range of motion on either side, it shows some restriction caused by adhesion formation. If only one side is restricted, mention it to your farrier to see what can be done.

When finished, take a close look at the shoe to see where the wear and tear of that particular shoe is showing. This also is a good indication of how the horse distributes his weight and uses that leg. You will be able to compare with the other leg and see the similarities or differences, if any.

*18.26* ***Holding the Hoof in a Neutral Position***

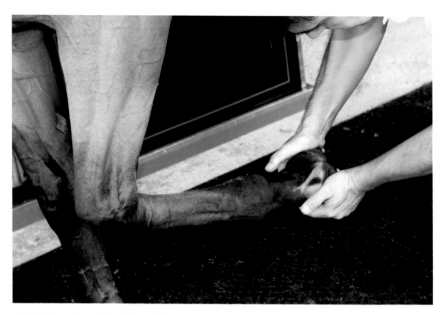

*18.27 **Rotating Hoof Laterally***

*18.28 **Rotating Hoof Medially***

## STRETCHING THE FORELEG

Stretching your horse's foreleg will further contribute to your evaluation. Please review figures 4.1 to 4.5 in chapter 4 for details on the various foreleg stretches you can perform with your animal.

If your horse feels restricted during his foreleg stretch, this can simply indicate some muscle tension. It can also reveal that the horse experiences some discomfort in his leg joints or ligaments. If you suspect this is the case, contact your veterinarian to investigate further.

Take note of all details during the stretching session of your horse so you will be able to compare forelegs. Do they stretch in the same capacity? Does your horse drop his scapula evenly on both sides? Does he feel more restricted with one of his forelegs?

## ASSOCIATED STRESS POINTS

Following the palpation of the skeletal features of the forelimb, proceed to survey the following muscle locations for potential stress points. (See chapter 5, pages 59–61, for the stress point location chart for better visualization.) Use gentle kneading massage movements to work the muscles, interspersed with effleurage massage movements. Use stroking movements to flow from one point to the other.

SP5 is found along the crest of the withers at the level of the ninth thoracic vertebra, by the insertion tendon of the spinalis dorsi muscle located in the deep layer, as shown in figure 18.29.

SP6, SP7, and SP8 are found on the withers by the origin tendon of the trapezius muscle (located in the superficial layer) and of the rhomboideus muscle located in the deep layer, as shown in figure 18.30.

SP9 is found in the superior aspect of the scapula by the origin tendon of the supraspinatus muscle located in the deep layer, as shown in figure 18.31.

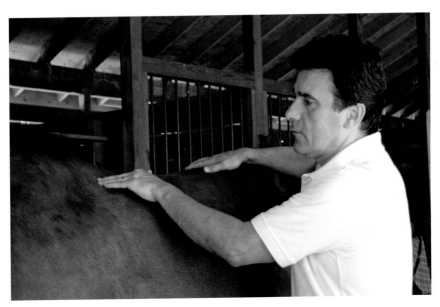

*18.29 Checking SP5*

*18.30 Checking SP6, SP7, and SP8*

*18.31 Checking SP9*

SP10 is found in the superior aspect of the scapula by the origin tendon of the infraspinatus muscle located in the deep layer, as shown in figure 18.32.

SP11 is found on the posterior aspect of the scapula by the insertion tendon of the serratus thoracis muscle located in the deep layer, as shown in figure 18.33.

SP12 is found on the medial aspect of the humerus, by the insertion tendon of the latissimus dorsi muscle located in the superficial layer, as shown in figure 18.34.

SP13 is found on the posterior edge of the scapula by the insertion tendon of the upper end of the triceps muscle located in the superficial layer, as shown in figure 18.35.

SP14 is found by the point of elbow, above the origin tendon of the triceps muscle located in the superficial layer, as shown in figure 18.36.

*18.32 Checking SP10*

*18.33 Checking SP11*

*18.34 Checking SP12*

*18.35 Checking SP13*

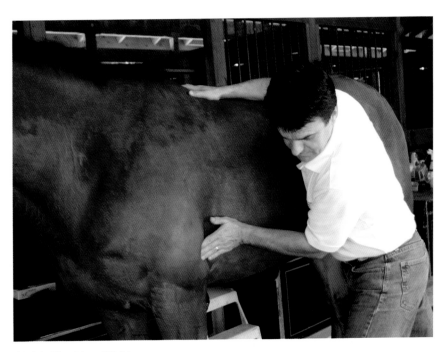

*18.36 Checking SP14*

SP15 is found on the medial aspect of the humerus, by the insertion tendon of the cranial superficial pectoral muscle located in the superficial layer, as shown in figure 18.37.

SP16 is found close to the sternum by the insertion tendon of the caudal superficial pectoral muscle located in the superficial layer, as shown in figure 18.38.

SP17 is found on the medial aspect of the humerus by the origin tendon of the caudal deep pectoral muscle located in the superficial layer, as shown in figure 18.39.

SP18 is found on the lateral aspect of the humerus, by the origin tendon of the radial carpal extensor muscles located in the superficial layer, as shown in figure 18.40. SP19 is found on the medial aspect of the ulna, by the origin tendon of the lateral carpal flexor muscles located in the superficial layer, as shown in figure 18.41.

Having a thorough knowledge of all the stress points found in the body of the horse will contribute tremendously to your evaluation.

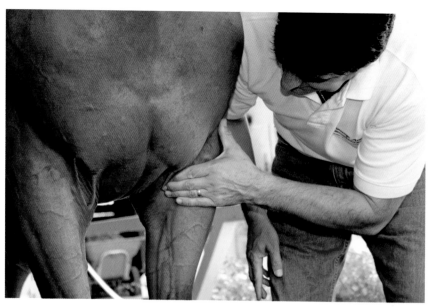

*18.37 Checking SP15*

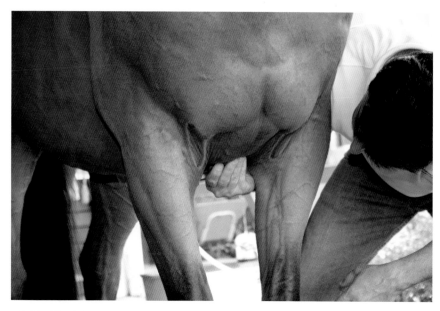

*18.38 Checking SP16*

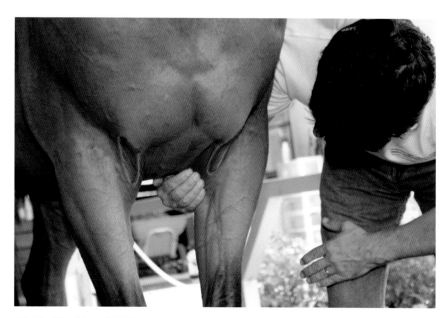

*18.39 Checking SP17*

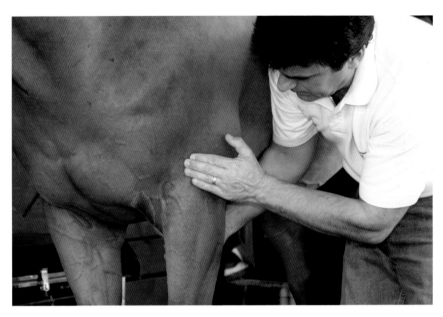

*18.40 Checking SP18*

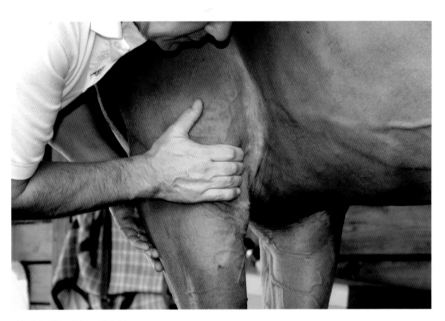

*18.41 Checking SP19*

# 19

The hind limb is made up of strong bones, ligaments, and muscles. The hind limbs' apparatus supplies most of the moving power needed for all gaits and for jumping. This is why you see the larger muscle groups and bones in the hind legs. Please take a moment to review figures 5.5, 5.8, 5.9, 5.11, 5.13, 5.14, and 5.15 in chapter 5 to refresh your memory of the actual location of these bones, ligaments, and muscles.

From conducting a massage palpation evaluation of points 20 to 25 over the hind limbs, you will be able to determine some very important components of the horse's health and performance:

The health of both hip (coxofemoral) joints: Healthy hips are important for the good translation of the power created by the powerful muscles of the hind legs to the rest of the body.

The health of a horse's stifles, hocks, fetlocks and pastern joints, and associated ligaments: Healthy joints in the hind legs are important to good motion and to create propulsion power.

Potential stress points in the hind legs' musculature: This information will help you better understand where your horse carries his stress and why.

Good conformation of the hind limbs is important. When standing behind the horse and looking at the leg as a whole, an ideal conformation structure can be identified by a theoretical perpendicular plumb line that should travel downward from the point of the tuber ischii, passing through the middle of the hock, the fetlock, and the hoof. (See chapter 6, page 66, for precise information on hind leg conformation.)

221

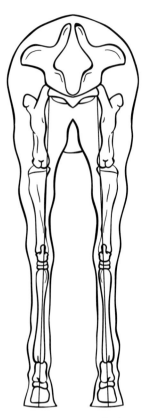

*19.1 **Hind Legs Ideal Caudal Plumb Line***

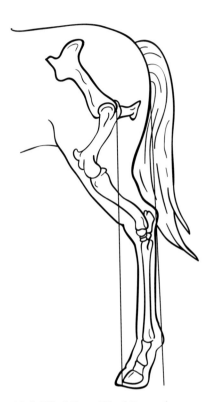

*19.2 **Hind Legs Ideal Lateral Plumb Line***

Good flexibility of the hind leg is vital to good performance. A horse uses his hind leg to power and balance the rest of his body. If any discomfort arises in either one of the hind limbs, it will quickly affect the rest of the body. Your massage palpation evaluation will allow you to identify areas of soreness and possibly inflammation along the various part of the hind leg.

As you start on one side, let your fingers' four T's give you direct feedback on the tonicity of the muscles and fascia tissues attaching over that area. When done, repeat the same procedure on the other side. Then compare your feedback sensations.

Start warming up the hindquarter with the SEW approach (see chapter 2, page 17). Follow with generous effleurages and move on to point 20.

As stated earlier, if you are with a young horse, he might be resistant to you grabbing his hind leg. Be careful and patient. Take the time to smile and praise him with your soft voice. It will make him relax and feel safe with you working his hind leg. The same might happen when you start stretching his hind leg. He might resist you a little at the very beginning, but he will surrender. Remember, if you are relaxed, he will relax.

## POINT 20: THE COXOFEMORAL JOINT

Checking the hip joint with your palpation skills will give you information on the following:

The quality of the gluteal muscles attaching onto the head of femur

The quality of the hamstring muscle group

The quality of the quadriceps muscle group

The tension in the local fascia layers

The level of inflammation in these structures, if any

Palpation of the point of coxofemoral joint is important because it might reveal tension and soreness of the various gluteus muscles, the quadriceps muscles, and/or of the femoral bursitis. The head of the femur should be well developed to provide solid anchoring to these muscles.

As shown in figure 19.3, couple your thumb, index, and major fingers. With a gentle friction-like action of your fingers, carefully work the greater trochanter of the head of femur.

This palpation will affect the tendon of insertion of the gluteus profondus and medius and the trochanteric bursa protecting the middle gluteus tendon over the greater trochanter of the femur. The trochanteric bursa often gets inflamed as a compensatory motion of the hinds for hock soreness or lameness. It gets quickly aggravated if the horse is asked

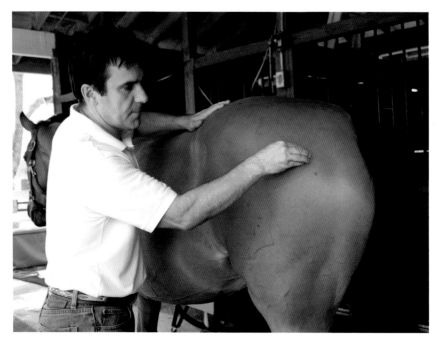

*19.3 Palpation of the Greater Trochanter of the Head of Femur*

to perform many turns, pirouettes, or half passes. Usually, an evaluation of the shoes will reveal that the inside wall of the shoe is more worn out than the outside. A trochanteric bursitis can also be secondary to a direct trauma (kick or blow).

Then keep gently frictioning while moving downward over the third (tertiary) trochanter, as shown in figure 19.4.

The third trochanter is where the superficial gluteus attaches. Soreness in this muscle indicates some degree of difficulty in the abduction of the hind leg.

If the horse flinches at any aspect of the trochanter, it reveals some soreness, possibly inflammation in the gluteus group, the primary leg retractor, and abductor muscle group of the hindquarters.

Palpate the hamstring group (semitendinosus, semimembranosus, biceps femoris) to evaluate the quality of their fibers, as shown in figure 19.5.

Hamstrings should be smooth. If you perceive firmness, or even hardness within the muscle bellies themselves, you are feeling adhesions (scar tissue). These adhesions limit the contraction powers of the muscle group. This condition is known as fibrotic and ossifying myopathy, and it affects the quality of movement in that muscle group, and restricts the horse's gait by causing shorter strides. This condition is common among horses in the western discipline. The sliding-to-stop motion predisposes these fibrotic lesions.

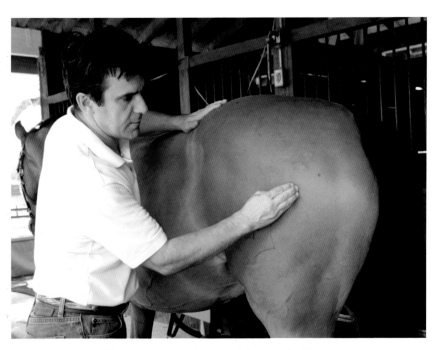

*19.4 Palpation of the Tertiary Trochanter of the Head of Femur*

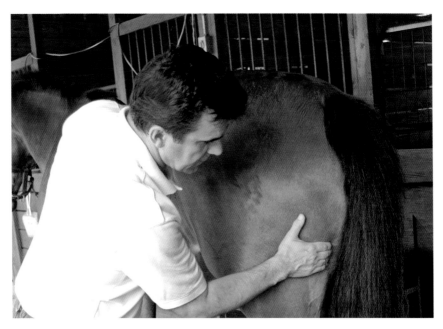

*19.5 Palpation of the Hamstring Muscle Group*

Next, move on to palpate the quadriceps muscle group of the thigh, as shown in figure 19.6.

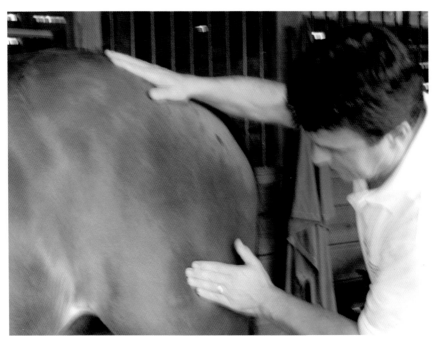

*19.6 Palpation of the Quadriceps Muscle Group of the Thigh*

The thigh should be long and well muscled. It has been pointed out that the greater the distance between the point of hip and the hock, the speedier the horse. Let your fingers' four T's give you direct feedback on the tonicity of the muscle and fascia tissues over the upper hind leg.

## POINT 21: THE STIFLE JOINT

Checking the stifle joint with your palpation skills will give you good information on the following:

The quality of the quadriceps muscle group attaching onto the stifle joint

The quality of the patellar ligaments attaching onto the stifle joint

The tension in the local fascia layers

The level of inflammation in these structures, if any

Position yourself properly to palpate the stifle, as shown in figure 19.7.

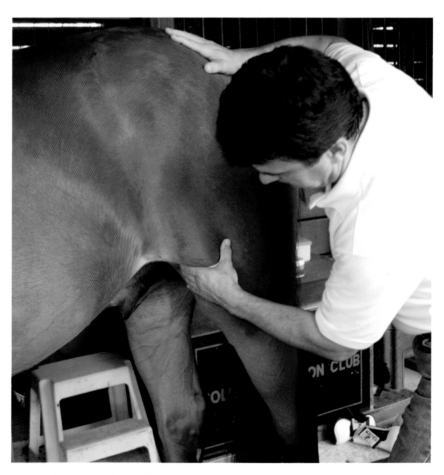

*19.7 Palpation of the Stifle Joint*

Palpation of the stifle joint is important because it might reveal soreness of the various tendons and ligaments that surround and support the stifle joint. The stifle should be well defined, with no bumps around the joint, and well forward in position. If the stifle feels hot or swollen, suspect either arthritis or some patellar problem.

Patellar problems usually develop on the medial aspect of the stifle joint with some swelling and some laxity of the collateral ligaments. Take the time to gently friction all the different ligaments attaching to the patella for a thorough evaluation: the prepatellar ligament and the medial and lateral patellar ligaments. If you perceive signs of inflammation on any aspect of the stifle, contact your veterinarian for further diagnosis

Move on to palpate the gaskin with some gentle friction movement, as shown in figure 19.8.

The gaskin should be strong since it is made of important muscles involved in the stifle and hock movements. As you gently friction the lower aspect of the stifle, pay particular attention to the horse's reaction. If you feel some excess tension over the dorsolateral aspect of the gaskin, it could indicate an old injury to the peroneus tertius, caused by an overextension of the hock. This is a common injury in thoroughbreds.

Let your fingers' four T's give you direct feedback on the tonicity of the muscles, tendons, and ligaments attaching over the stifle joint and upper hock.

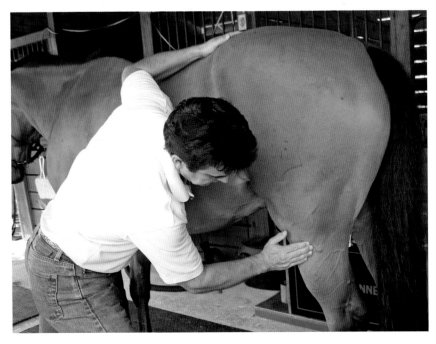

*19.8 Palpation of the Gaskin*

# POINT 22: THE HOCK JOINT

Checking the hock joint with your palpation skills will give you precise and precious information on the following:

The quality of the flexor and extensor tendons going by the hock joint

The quality of the retinaculum surrounding the hock joint

The tension in the local fascia layers

The level of inflammation in these structures, if any

This joint is very important in the propulsion of the horse. Position yourself properly to palpate the hock, as shown in figure 19.9.

The hock should be strong and wide with a clean outline, and flat on the sides with a rounded point at the back known as the tuber calcanei. A well-developed hock should be big in proportion to the size of the horse.

Look for any bony growth at the lower and inner front of the hock, as shown in figure 19.10.

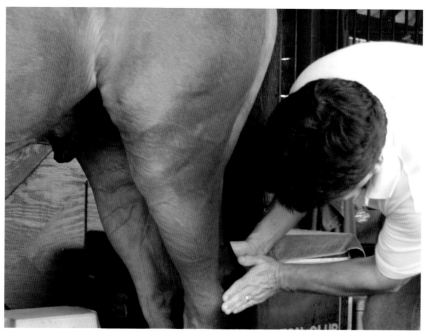

*19.9 Palpation of the Hock Laterally*

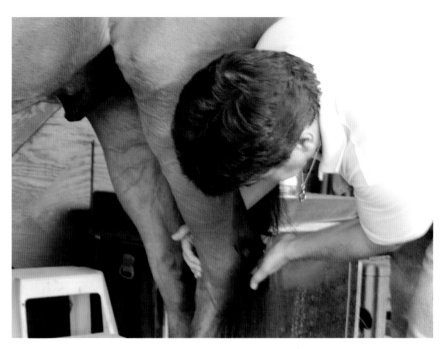

*19.10 Palpation of the Hock Medially*

Your palpation might reveal a spavin condition, a bony enlargement resulting from a degenerative joint condition causing lameness. If you feel some inflammatory symptoms of heat and swelling on the lower medial aspect of the hock, suspect a bog spavin condition, where the synovial membrane of the hock has become unduly distended. If you feel some inflammatory symptoms of heat and swelling in front of the hock, suspect some arthritis. If the inflammation is located medially at the lower aspect of the hock, suspect a cunean bursitis. In any case, you should contact your veterinarian for proper supervision.

Switch positions to evaluate the posterior aspect of the hock, as shown in figure 19.11.

If you feel some inflammatory symptoms of heat and swelling behind the hock, suspect a curb condition (the tearing of ligaments), a thoroughpin condition (inflammation of the synovial sheath of the deep flexor tendon), a capped hock condition (inflammation of the bursa between the skin and the calcis bone of the tuber calcanei), or possibly some osteochondrosis of the hock (inflammation of the cartilage of the hock). An old case of luxation of the hock could also leave some chronic soreness, possibly chronic inflammation symptoms.

Let your fingers' four T's give you direct feedback on the tonicity of the muscle, ligament, and fascia tissues attaching over the hock joint.

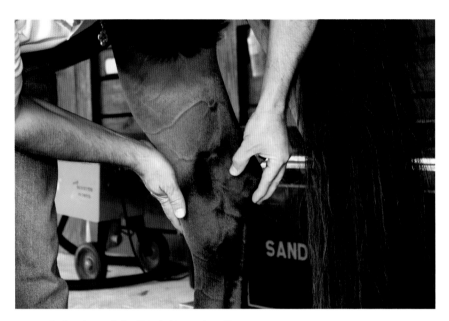

*19.11 Palpation of the Hock Posteriorly*

When done with your palpation, step back behind the horse to get an overall view of the hocks. They might be close together (cow hocks) or wide apart (bowed hocks). Both conditions indicate a slight weakness in the leg structure that can lead to complications such as thoroughpin or bog spavin condition.

## FETLOCK, PASTERN, AND DIGIT OF THE HIND LIMB

To check the rest of the lower aspect of the hind leg, proceed as you did for the lower foreleg. The conformation points and characteristics in the lower hind limb are essentially the same as in the forelimb. The suspensory apparatus and the digital flexor tendons are very similar to those of the forelimb. However, there are a few anatomical differences, such as:

The articular angle of the fetlock is about 5 degrees sharper in the hind limb than in the forelimb.

The inclination of the dorsal surface of the hoof is usually about 5 degrees sharper than that of the forelimb.

The phalanxes are slightly narrower and longer than in the forelimb.

The inferior check ligament originating on the plantar aspect of the hock is much weaker than its forelimb counter part.

The hind foot's shape is usually narrower than the forefoot.

When working on the hind leg, consider using the posture shown in figure 19.12. I call it the farrier position. This approach will keep the pressure off your back and allow you to keep your hands free to work as you please.

You might encounter a horse who has difficulty with that position. This can be due to tight hip flexor muscles, the iliopsoas muscle group, or some sore stifle or hock joints, possibly the lumbar spine. Do not force the animal into that stretch if he resists. Sometimes, the newness of this approach is what causes the horse to resist. In that case, adjust to the posture shown in figure 19.13.

Then stroke the flexor tendon to relax the horse and induce a better stretch, as shown in figure 19.14.

Very often, this will suffice to gain the horse's confidence and for him to stretch out his hind leg without resistance.

# POINT 23: THE SUSPENSORY LIGAMENT AND THE FLEXOR TENDON

To check the lower aspect of the hind leg, proceed as you did for the lower foreleg (see chapter 18, page 201). The conformation points and characteristics are essentially the same. However, you might want to use the posture shown in figure 19.15 to proceed with your palpation.

*19.12 Position to Evaluate the Lower Hind Leg (Farrier Position)*

*19.13 Farrier Position with Contracted Hind Leg*

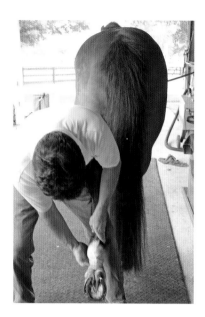

*19.14 Farrier Position, Stroking the Flexor Tendon*

*19.15 Position to Evaluate the Tendon and Ligament of Lower Hind Leg*

## POINT 24: THE FETLOCK

Place your hands as shown in figure 19.16 to proceed with your palpation of the collateral ligaments of the hind leg's fetlock. Then, as shown in figure 19.17, check the sesamoid bones in a similar fashion as for the lower foreleg since the conformation points and characteristics are essentially the same (see chapter 18, page 201).

## POINT 25: THE PASTERN BONES AND HOOF

Check the pasterns and hoof of the hind leg, using the posture shown in figure 19.18. Then check the lateral cartilages, as shown in figure 19.19. Since the conformation points and characteristics are essentially the same than those of the foreleg, refer to chapter 18, page 201, for details.

Check the flexion and extension of the hoof, as shown respectively in figures 19.20 and 19.21

Next, check for the lateral rotation of the hoof around the axis of the pasterns. Start by holding the hoof in a neutral position and then rotate laterally and then medially, as shown respectively in figures 19.22, 19.23, and 19.24.

**19.16** *Position to Evaluate the Collateral Ligament of the Fetlock of Lower Hind Leg*

**19.17** *Position to Evaluate the Sesamoid Bones of Fetlock of Lower Hind Leg*

**19.18** *Position to Evaluate the Pastern and Hoof of Lower Hind Leg*

**19.19** *Position to Evaluate the Hoof Lateral Cartilages*

*19.20 Flexion of Hoof*

*19.21 Extension of Hoof*

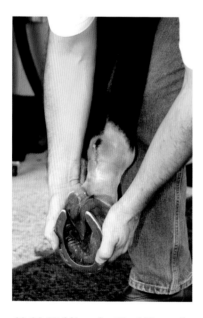

*19.22 Holding the Hoof Neutral*

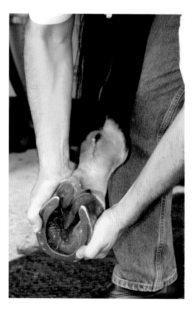

*19.23 Rotating the Hoof Laterally*

*19.24 Rotating the Hoof Medially*

As mentioned earlier with the foreleg, take a close look at the shoe to see where the wear and tear of that particular shoe is showing. It reveals how the horse distributes his weight and uses that leg. Compare with the other leg. Note the similarities or differences, if any.

### STRETCHING THE HIND LEG

Stretching your horse's hind leg will further contribute to your evaluation. How the horse responds to each stretch will indicate limb flexibility, or lack thereof. Please review figures 4.6 to 4.10 in chapter 4 for details on the various hind leg stretches you can perform with your animal.

If your horse appears restricted during his hind leg stretch this may simply be due to some muscle tension. It can also reveal some discomfort in the hind leg joints or ligaments. If you suspect that is the case, please contact your veterinarian for further investigation. Otherwise, are both hind legs stretching to the same extent? Does your horse favor one leg?

## ASSOCIATED STRESS POINTS

Following the palpation of the skeletal features of the forelimb, proceed to supervise the following muscle locations for potential stress points. Refer to chapter 5, pages 59–61, for the stress point location chart for better visualization. Use gentle kneading massage movements to work the muscles, effleurage massage movements to drain, and stroking movements to flow from one point to the other.

SP27 is found a few inches away from the spine at the level of the second and third lumbar vertebrae, by the junction fascia of the gluteus muscle (located in the superficial layer) and the longissimus dorsi muscle located in the superficial layer, as shown in figure 19.25.

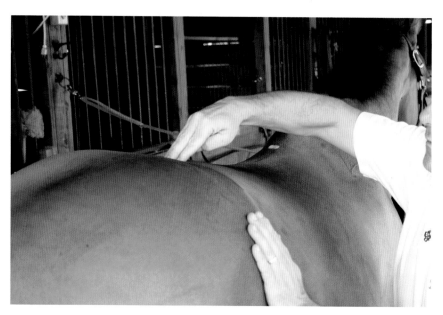

*19.25 Checking SP27*

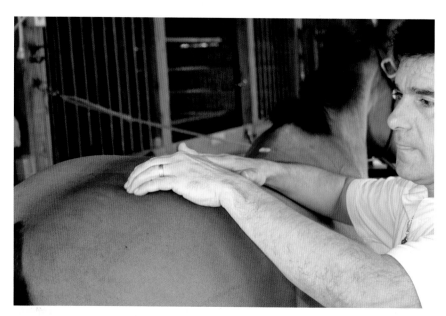

*19.26 Checking SP28*

SP28 is found by the sacrum, just below the origin tendon of the biceps femoris muscle located in the superficial layer, as shown in figure 19.26.

SP29 is found above the gaskin (the tibia bone) at the bifurcation of the biceps femoris muscle located in the superficial layer, as shown in figure 19.27.

SP30 is found above the hock joint, before the insertion tendon of the gastrocnemius muscle located in the deep layer, as shown in figure 19.28.

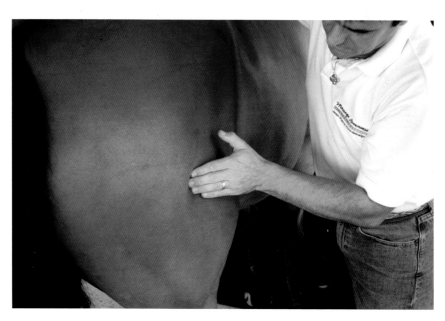

*19.27 Checking SP29*

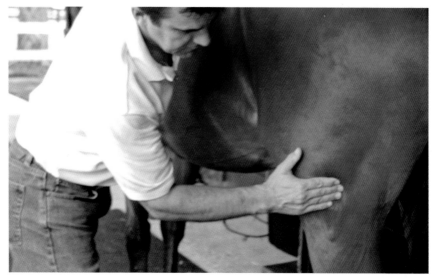

*19.28 Checking SP30*

SP31 is found by the stifle joint, above the insertion tendon of the vastus lateralis muscle located in the deep layer, as shown in figure 19.29.

SP32 is found by the stifle joint, above the insertion tendon of the rectus femoris muscle located in the deep layer, as shown in figure 19.30.

SP33 is found by the stifle joint, above the insertion tendon of the adductor muscles located in the deep layer, as shown in figure 19.31.

*19.29 Checking SP31*

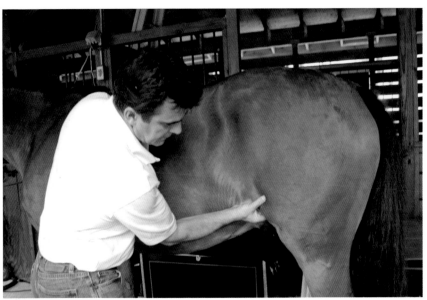

*19.30 Checking SP32*

SP34 is found by the sacrum, below the origin tendon of the semi-tendinosus muscle located in the superficial layer, as shown in figure 19.32.

SP35 is found by the sacrum, below the insertion tendon of the semi-membranosus muscle located in the superficial layer, as shown in figure 19.33.

SP36 is found by the point of hip, below the origin tendon of the tensor fascia latae muscle located in the superficial layer, as shown in figure 19.34.

*19.31 Checking SP33*

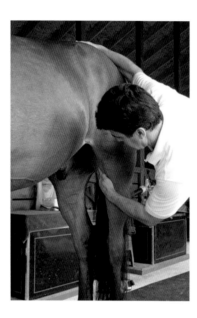

*19.32 Checking SP34*

*19.33 Checking SP35*          *19.34 Checking SP36*

SP37 is found by the iliac crest, below the origin tendon of the iliacus muscle located in the deep layer, as shown in figure 19.35.

SP38 is found a couple inches from the point of hip, by the origin tendon of the superficial gluteus muscle located in the superficial layer, as shown in figure 19.36.

SP39 is found on the lateral aspect of the tibia by the origin tendon of the long digital extensor muscles located in the superficial layer, as shown in figure 19.37.

SP40 is found on the medial aspect of the fibula by the origin tendon of the long digital flexor muscles located in the superficial layer, as shown in figure 19.38.

Having a thorough knowledge of all the stress points found in the body of the horse will contribute tremendously to your evaluation.

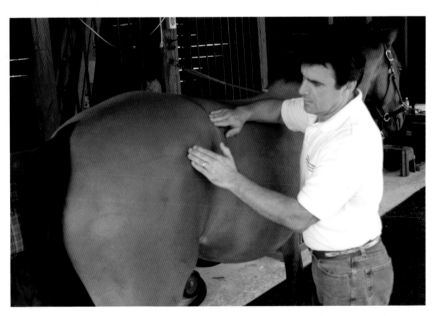

*19.35 Checking SP37*

*19.36 Checking SP38*

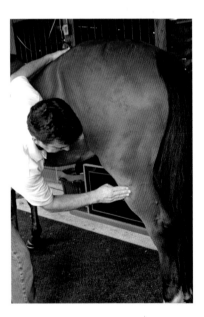

*19.37 Checking SP39*

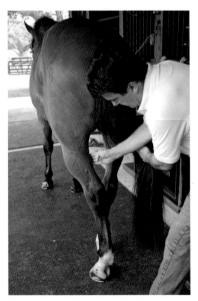

*19.38 Checking SP40*

# 20

This multipoint palpation evaluation program gives you a chance to regularly check the musculoskeletal fitness of your horse. If your horse is sound, great! Keep on training and improving. On the other hand, if you detect any abnormalities, signs of inflammation, or when simply in doubt, contact your veterinarian immediately for proper diagnosis and course of action.

Regular application of this PEP will serve you well. It will help you stay on top of your horse's musculoskeletal fitness, giving you an opportunity to take action immediately and to prevent discomfort to your horse, not to mention costly delays. Practice makes perfect. Contact the author for further information on training clinics and other learning tools.

To help you take notes during your PEP, use the following chart.

| PALPATION EVALUATION PROGRAM | |
|---|---|
| **BODY PART** | **COMMENTS** |
| 1. The teeth and mandible | |
| 2. The temporomandibular joint (TMJ) | |
| 3. The occipital bone of the skull and the first cervical vertebra area (C0-C1) | |
| 4. The second to fifth cervical vertebrae area (C2-C3-C4-C5) | |
| 5. The sixth and seventh cervical vertebrae (C6-C7) | |
| 6. The withers (thoracic spinous processes – T5-T11) | |
| 7. The back (thoracic spine) | |
| 8. The rib cage | |
| 9. The lower back (lumbar spine) | |
| 10. The sacrum | |
| 11. The tail | |
| 12. The hip | |
| 13. The scapula and its muscle sling | |

| PALPATION EVALUATION PROGRAM *(continued)* | |
|---|---|
| **BODY PART** | **COMMENTS** |
| 14. The point of shoulder | |
| 15. The elbow joint | |
| 16. The knee joint | |
| 17. The canon bone, suspensory ligament, and flexor tendon | |
| 18. The fetlock joint | |
| 19. The pasterns and hoof | |
| 20. The coxofemoral (hip) joint | |
| 21. The stifle joint | |
| 22. The hock joint | |
| 23. The suspensory ligament and flexor tendon | |
| 24. The fetlock | |
| 25. The pasterns and hoof | |

This summary chart will help you write all the important details picked up during your PEP, so when conversing with your veterinarian or your trainer, you will have all the information at hand.

# Conclusion

This fitness evaluation program of the horse is a great routine you can use at any time, anywhere, and on any horse. Both the riding evaluation program (REP) and the palpation evaluation program (PEP) will reveal a lot of information about the horse. The combination of these two tests will allow you to find out about:

- ❖ Any dentition problem
- ❖ Any skeletal problem
- ❖ Any existing musculoskeletal condition or conformation problem
- ❖ Any weak body part
- ❖ Any achy legs from the wear and tear on joints
- ❖ Any discomfort from the effect of the present shoeing

From there you can choose the best course of action to improve the fitness of your horse. Depending upon your findings, you might simply need to adjust your training program in order to remedy the possible weakness at hand, or you might need to call upon other professionals to help your horse back to better musculoskeletal fitness.

In the case of evaluating a potential new horse, your personal examination will reveal right away whether this particular horse is a good candidate. If, from your personal fitness evaluation program, you feel that the horse presents some serious musculoskeletal issues that would interfere with your riding goals, then you can reconsider your decision, and you have just saved yourself a bunch of time and money.

On the other end, if the horse appears to be a good candidate, then you can move to the next step: contracting a veterinarian for a prepurchase examination. Through your veterinarian's findings, he or she will be able to inform and advise you about the horse's complete general health and about any specific condition the horse may present.

Understanding these facts will help you make the right decision for you. It is important you understand the difference between conformation faults that are manageable and will not affect the horse's performance and those that will affect his performance.

It is thus very important to select a horse who will match your expectations with a suited conformation, with good shoes, with ample freedom of movement (meaning showing as little bone, joint, and muscular restriction as possible), and with steadiness in his gaits, so that the horse can benefit from all his potential. With time and your training, you will be able to improve your horse and help him reach his optimal performance.

A horse's breeding, conformation, and training influence the way he moves. Each discipline favors certain ways of moving and certain gaits. Discussing each and every breed and discipline is beyond the scope of this book. Regardless of the gait and flavor of the moment, soundness of the horse and a good work ethic are of the utmost importance.

As much as this test will help you identify the fitness level of your horse, it will also help you discover your horse's demeanor and work ethic.

- ❖ Is your horse willing to work?
- ❖ Is he showing good temperament?
- ❖ Does he enjoy working?
- ❖ Is he lazy or erratic?
- ❖ Is he temperamental?

This thorough test will help you discover all those details so you can choose the right horse for you.

# Index